Captain Corelli's Island

Captain Corelli's Island

Island

CEPHALLONIA

Andy Harris
Photographs by Terry Harris

PAVILION

First published in Great Britain in 1999 by

PAVILION BOOKS LIMITED

London House, Great Eastern Wharf, Parkgate Road, London SW11 4NQ

Designed by Andrew Barron & Collis Clements Associates

Cartography by David Williams

A CIP catalogue record for this book is available
from the British Library.

ISBN 1 86205 306 5

Set in Bernhard Modern and News Gothic

Printed in Italy by Conti Tipocolor

Colour origination in England by Alliance Graphics

2 4 6 8 10 9 7 5 3 1

This book can be ordered direct from the publisher. Please contact
the Marketing Department. But try your bookshop first.

Contents

Acknowledgements from Terry Harris

My thanks to Spiros Kapatsoris, Gerassimos Adonatos,
Pater Arsenios, Alkiviadis Pefanis, Costas and Elenanthi Mercato
and everyone else in Cephallonia who helped me.

Also to Panos Argyros, Sue Stewart
and Andy McDowell.

Right:
**An old postcard
showing the
entrance to the
Napier Gardens in
Argostoli.**
Half-title page:
A Greek flag
Title page:
**One of the boats
used to row visitors
into the Melissani
caves**

Introduction

History is indelibly etched on to the barren rocks of all the Greek islands. A few sun-bleached marble columns of an ancient temple; the mossy foundations of an abandoned Byzantine church; a crumbling Venetian watch-tower on a windswept headland; or the rusting frame of a crashed Second World War fighter plane; all are revealing clues to the often turbulent pasts of the islands. Sometimes hard to decipher amidst the rash of modern tourist hotels and villas that have been built in recent years, such scars often remain the only archaeological links on the rapidly changing island landscapes; mysterious threads that help unwind their sometimes tortuous histories.

The islands have been fought over ever since the Minoan and Mycenaean civilizations first established colonies on them in the Bronze Age. Other empire-builders, most notably the Venetians and Ottomans, squabbled over their agricultural and mineral riches, or sought to control them in order to take advantage of their strategic position on Mediterranean trade routes. Finally, in the late nineteenth century, came the birth of modern Greece. It was a process that was to continue until 1948, when the Dodecanese islands became part of Greece, and the country's geographical borders were finally defined as they are known today.

Cephallonia itself has a fascinating and tragic tale to tell. In mythology it was part of Odysseus's legendary kingdom; in antiquity its four city states grew rich from trade until the Romans took the island in the second century BC. Always a prized jewel in the crowns of its many conquerors, its forests of unique Cephallonian pine supplied the shipyards of ancient Greece and Venice, and its vineyards of 'black gold' (currants) brought great wealth to French and British merchants. It has been hideaway or home to pirates and poets, such as Barbarossa and Byron. The

Opposite:
Zoodochous Pigi Church: Spiros Frangopoulos singing Cephallonian Cantades after a religious festival

8

Left:
**An old postcard of
Argostoli**

unnecessary massacre of Italian troops by the Germans at the end of the Second World War, and the destructive 1953 earthquake, are two bitter incidents that have scarred the island psyche. In recent decades it has followed the course of the entire Aegean archipelago, as tourism and Greece's entry into the European Community have given its inhabitants some new-found wealth.

The islanders themselves have long been known for their fighting prowess and intelligence, producing great warriors, poets, politicians and sea captains. Travelling the world, many came to prominence in unusual places, such as Constantine Yerakis who became prime minister of Siam in the seventeenth century. Writing in 1890, Joseph Partsch, a German geographer who travelled throughout the island said, 'The Cephallonians would have been the Prussians of Greece had there been more of them.'

The largest of the Ionian islands, Cephallonia's 277 square miles offer a rough-and-tumble drive through a dramatic landscape of forest-clad mountains and hidden valleys, impressive limestone caves and cliffs, spacious bays reached by tortuous narrow roads. Racked and ruined by severe earthquakes throughout its history, little remains of its former architectural glory today. The last earthquake has left an eerie legacy of abandoned, ghostly homes in countless villages and towns across the island.

As the setting for Louis de Bernières' best-selling novel *Captain Corelli's Mandolin*, the island has also gained an unexpected notoriety in the past few years, with a steady trickle of new visitors, all searching for the sights and sounds revealed in the novel. There have been few such charming depictions of modern Greek island life and history as *Captain Corelli's Mandolin*, and this book only hopes to complement the novel's successful evocation.

Overleaf:
**A view of Lixouri
with Mount Aenos
in the distance**

Ancient History

Cephallonia's ancient history is an often heady mix of fact and fiction. Mythology creates countless genealogical inconsistencies; and when archaeology has attempted to answer many of the early chronological confusions, it has always been hampered by centuries of relentless seismic activity, which has reduced most of the island's remaining ruins to little more than heaps of rubble. Earthquakes on the island in 1636 and 1953, in particular, destroyed many important antiquities.

Early inhabitants

Finds from the palaeolithic period trace the first inhabitants to *circa* 50,000 BC. But some of the flint tools and fossilized animal bones, dated to an even earlier period, provide evidence that the island was one of the first inhabited areas of Greece. Such remains, found in abundance around Poros, Skala, Fiskardo and Sami, are always open to interpretation without accurate dating techniques. After excavating a site at Fiskardo in 1984, the archaeologist George Kavadias established that some of his impressive collection of obsidian and flint axes, scrapers and arrowheads dated from 80,000 BC. These can now be seen in Argostoli's Archaeological Museum. However, another eminent Cephallonian archaeologist, the late Spyros Marinatos (discoverer of Santorini's Akrotiri), believes that most of these finds are more likely to belong to the mesolithic and neolithic periods (10,000–7000 BC).

According to Greek mythology, the island's first recorded inhabitants were the Taphians or Teleboans. In some early accounts, either an area near Lixouri or the island as a whole was known as 'Taphios' after its first ruler, Taphios, descended from King Perseus of Mycenae. Led by his son Pterelaus, the Taphians demanded part of King Electryon's Mycenaean

Opposite:
Above Sami on a pine-clad hill stand the ruins of the acropolis of Cyatis, all that remains of the ancient city of Sami

kingdom. When he refused, they stole his herd of oxen. Enraged, Electryon enlisted the help of Amphitryon, the King of Thebes, to conquer them. Assisted by Cephalos and Heleios, the Taphians were defeated. Both of these warrior heroes were given different parts of the island kingdom as a reward. Some historians place Cephalos's kingdom around Lakithra and Metaxata's antiquities in the Livatho area. Heleios's is sited at Mavrata, in a southern area of the island still called Elios.

Another popular myth sees Cephalos alone give his name to the island, forced into exile on Cephallonia, after accidentally killing his wife Prokris in a hunting accident in Attica. Cephalos had been happily married to Prokris, the daughter of King Erechtheus, until Eos, the goddess of dawn, became enamoured of him. Unable to quell Cephalos's love for Prokris, Eos craftily questioned his wife's fidelity. In order to test her, Cephalos disguised himself as a suitor and, bearing gifts, he returned and successfully wooed Prokris before revealing his true identity. Stricken with grief, Prokris escaped to Crete, where King Minos promptly fell in love with her. Hiding out in the island's mountains, and afraid of more extramarital strife from Minos's wife, she became an accomplished huntress. The goddess Artemis, taking pity on her, gave her Laelaps, a hunting dog, and a spear that always found its mark, before sending her home to Cephalos. Still jealous of Eos, Prokris followed her husband everywhere until the final tragedy occurred. Hiding in some bushes on a hunting expedition, Cephalos mistook her for a deer, killing her with Artemis's faultless spear.

To confuse matters even further, other writers give alternative versions of the myth. Aristotle tells us how Cephalos, who could not have children, went to consult the Oracle of Delphi. The priestess told him to make love

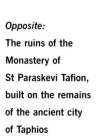

with the first female creature that he saw. It turned out to be a bear, which is how Arceisios, the future King of Acarnania, was born. His son Laertes was Odysseus's father, which neatly ties the myth's hereditary lineage back to the island.

There is also some debate about whether the island's name derives from this hero, or from the fact that its inhabitants were descended from the Kefallines, the people of Cephallonia, Itháki, Zakynthos, Lefkada and parts of Acarnania ruled over by Odysseus, that Homer mentions for the first time in the *Iliad*. What is clear from all these early genealogical references is that the first settlers, whether they were the Taphians or Kefallines, who both originated from western Greece, worshipped all these relevant gods and demigods. Early coins found on the island feature Cephalos, Prokris, Laelaps, Poseidon (also supposedly Taphios's father), Athena (Odysseus's ally) and Demeter (goddess of agriculture).

By 1300 BC, Mycenaean culture was flourishing on the island, introduced by the Achaeans from Arcadia in the central Peloponnese. Dozens of their battered skulls have been found in the Lakithra tombs. Studies show many of them to have fractures that had healed, proving that they were hardy warriors with conquistador tendencies. The abundance of rock-hewn beehive tombs at Lakithra, Livatho, Kokolata, Mazarakata, Parisata, Mavrata, Diakata, Kontogenada, Tzanata and Grania, filled with significant artifacts and votive offerings, also confirms the importance of this Mycenaean civilization. From this time, the island was divided into four separate fortified city states, and called a 'Tetrapolis' by Thucydides. The four states – Krane, Pronoi, Pale and Same, said to take their names from Cephalos's children – prospered until the Hellenistic period.

During the Trojan War, Same was the most important and powerful

Opposite:
**Wild flowers
surround the fields
and cliffs of the
Assos peninsula**

city state. In mythology, its ruler was Angaios, one of Zeus's descendants and an important Arcadian hero. According to Aristotle, he was an enthusiastic agriculturalist and the first to extensively cultivate vineyards on the island. Homer confuses matters by calling the whole island Sami or Samos, when he tells of Odysseus taking twelve ships to Troy from 'glittering Samos' filled with 'big-hearted Kefallines'. He also mentions that most of Penelope's suitors came from Same and Doulikhion. Although scholars argue endlessly about Homeric geography, it is clear that Doulikhion was Pale. Herodotus, in 450 BC, is the first to refer to the island by its more modern name of Kefallini.

There is not much recorded information from the archaic and classical periods between 1100–800 BC. The four cities wavered continually between Corinth and Athens, who fought over the island's strategic importance as the final port on their sea routes to Magna Graecia, especially the colonies in southern Italy and Sicily. There is evidence of temples and sanctuaries, the earliest dating from the sixth century BC, along the island coastline at Kapri, Skala, Perachora, Leukata and Valtsa, where their ships would stop to pay homage to various gods. The cities also developed culturally. In 582 BC, during the 48th Olympiad at the Pythia games in Delphi, a Cephallonian called Melampous won the lyre and song contest, proving that there was a strong musical heritage on the island.

Hesiod also mentions a famous sanctuary on the island, dedicated to Zeus, lying just east and ten feet below the summit of Mount Aenos.

Left:
Beneath the Agrillion Monastery hidden in the hills above Sami, Anti Samos Bay is a beautiful sandy beach reached by a dirt-track road and rimmed by trees

Numerous animal bones and pottery shards have been found at the site. It is said that its priests made sacrifices when they saw the smoke from the altar sacrifices of the temple of Thios on the small island of modern-day Dias. Sadly, earthquakes have destroyed the remains of the temple of Thios. When the English traveller D.T. Ansted visited the mountain site in 1863, he observed: 'Here above remain the stones of the altar and the burnt bones of the bulls and goats; there below, at a distance of several miles, the more solid and beautiful temple is gone – not one stone remains upon another, and there is nothing but the story, probable enough for that matter, to connect the two localities.' Another Doric temple was known at Krane. Dedicated to Demeter, its remains are said to be in the Koutavos lagoon beneath the ancient city's fortifications. In Argostoli's Archaeological Museum, there is one remnant – a temple inscription that is a dedication from a Cephallonian woman called Triopis to Demeter and Kora.

In 479 BC, Pale sent 200 warriors to help Athens defeat the Persians at the Battle of Plataea. Siding with the Corinthians in 435 BC, the city sent four ships in the unsuccessful fight against the Corcyraeans of modern-day Corfu. During the Peloponnesian War (431–404 BC) all four cities allied themselves to Athens, which used the island as a base for its fleet's attacks on Corinth. When the Corinthians sent forty ships and

Right:
Opposite Avithos beach is the tiny islet of Dias, site of the ancient temple of Thios destroyed by the incessant earthquakes, and behind it the island of Zakynthos

1,500 warriors to Krane, the city pretended to negotiate with them before routing the invaders. In 404 BC, at the end of the Peloponnesian War, the cities sided with Sparta. After Athens had defeated the Spartans, Pronoi and Pale joined the Second Athenian Confederacy formed in 375 BC. When Philip II of Macedon conquered Greece in 337 BC, the cities allied themselves to the Macedonians. At the Battle of Lamia in 323–322 BC, after the sudden death of Alexander the Great in 323 BC when the Greeks tried to end Macedonian rule, the cities remained loyal to the Macedonians. In 226 BC they joined the Aetolian League, joining in the attack and plundering of the Achaean kingdoms. In 218 BC Philip V of Macedonia, allied to the Achaeans, attempted and failed to conquer the island.

The Roman conquest of Greece

When Rome began its relentless conquest of Greece in 200 BC, defeating Philip V in 197 BC, the Ionian islands were among the first to fall, strategically vital to the Romans' eventual attack on Corinth and the mainland. Corfu was first, followed by Zakynthos, and Cephallonia which finally fell in 189 BC. The Roman consul Marcus Fulvius Nobili asked the four cities to surrender and each hand over twenty prominent citizens as hostages. Same was the only city that immediately closed its city gates. Besieged by the Roman forces, it put up a heroic resistance. This is Livy's account of the attack:

'Samos supported a siege of four months. At last, as some of their small number were killed or wounded daily, and the survivors were, through continual fatigues, greatly reduced both in strength and spirits, the Romans, one night, scaling the walls of the citadel which they call

Opposite:
Founded in 1759, the Monastery of Kipourion has a dramatic cliff-top setting, and is home to various miraculous icons

Cyatides, made their way into the forum. The Samians, on discovering that a part of the city was taken, fled, with their wives and children, into the greater citadel; but submitting next day, they were all sold as slaves, and their city was plundered.'

Life under the yolk of the Roman empire was hard. Around 50 BC, when Caius Antonius, brother of the famous Mark Antony, was exiled to the island, it became little more than his private estate. He was beginning to build a new town but received an amnesty in 72 BC, enabling him to return to political life in Rome. Some remains from this occupation have been found in Skala and Sami. A villa in Skala, dating from the third century AD, reveals two mosaic floors in good condition, executed by the artist Crateros. One depicts a sacrifice, known as *suovetaurilia*, of three male animals (a boar, a ram and an ox). In Sami, a bath has been unearthed with a mosaic floor decorated with geometric patterns. In Argostoli's Archaeological Museum, there is also a fragment of a mosaic from Valtsa of Poseidon with his trident, and an impressive bronze head

from a life-sized statue found in the Sami bathhouse. It is thought to be of Epithanes, an early Gnostic honoured in Same because his mother was born there.

From Byzantium to French Rule

By the time of the Emperor Constantine in the fourth century AD, the Roman Empire was in a state of diffusion and decline, weakened by attacks from Arab pirates around the Mediterranean, and from marauding Goths who remained a constant threat on its northern borders. When Constantine reorganized the Empire in 323 AD, by laying the foundations for the city of Constantinople and ultimately the Byzantine Empire, Cephallonia came under the rule of the eparchy of Achaea as a part of the Eastern Roman Empire. On the death of the Emperor Theodosius I in 395 AD, the Roman Empire was formally divided into the Greek-speaking East and Latin-speaking West; an act that allowed the gradual formation of the Byzantine Empire as Constantinople established its importance over Rome as a capital city.

After the Slavs attacked Crete in 623 AD, the Emperor Heraclius reorganized the Empire once again into a smaller, and more manageable, number of themes (administrative districts), able to respond quickly to the Arab attacks that were frequent at the time. Cephallonia joined the Eleventh Theme of Longobardia (Lombardy), benefiting from their strong naval superiority when Saracen pirates attacked the island. When Nicephorus I (802–809 AD) came to power, the island then became part of the Theme of Calabria.

During Leo the Wise's reign in 887 AD, the island's importance was recognized when he transformed it into its own independent theme. The Theme of Cephallonia, with its capital at Pale, oversaw all the other Ionian islands except Kythera, and was a crucial defensive outpost of the Empire. With its new-found authority it prospered. When Nicephorus Phocas defeated the Arabs in Crete in 961 AD, reasserting Byzantine maritime supremacy in the Aegean, and banishing the pirate threat for

Opposite:
Avithos beach is also the site of an annual celebration on 2 July when locals celebrate the Panagia Vlachernon chapel feast day. The chapel was rebuilt after the 1953 earthquake by the Vallianos ship-owning family

Opposite:

**Fiskardo's
19th-century
neo-classical sea
captain's mansions,
painted in faded
pink and ochre
colours, were
unscathed by the
1953 earthquake**

another 100 years, the island continued to flourish until the arrival of the Normans.

The rule of the Normans

Using the pretext of the Crusades, the aggressive Normans, under their leaders, the brothers Robert and Roger Guiscard, began also ultimately to threaten the Byzantine Empire. Sweeping through Italy, they conquered Rome in 1053, Otranto in 1055 and Sicily in 1071. A decade later, they were marching on Greece and Constantinople. In 1081, their fleet attacked the Ionian islands and successfully attacked Corfu. In 1082, Cephallonia proved harder to conquer, when the Norman force failed to take the fortified city of Pale. An elderly Robert Guiscard sailed to their rescue, anchoring off Cape Panormos at the northern tip of the island, only to die of a fever on board his ship within sight of the ancient town of Athera. Modern-day Fiskardo, a corruption of Guiscard, takes its name from the unsuccessful duke.

Ultimately, the duke's timely death deprived the Normans of the Emperor Alexius's throne. It was only a matter of time, and honour, before the Normans attacked again. On the way back from the First Crusade, Robert's son Bohemond, avenged his father's death by cruelly sacking Cephallonia. During this period, from the end of the eleventh century through to the latter half of the twelfth century, when the Byzantine Empire was under attack from all sides, the island was briefly conquered also by two other greedy seafaring states, the Pisans and the Venetians.

The Emperor Alexius's son, John Comnenus (1118–43) tried in vain to enlist the Pope's support against the ever restless Normans in Sicily, under Robert Guiscard's nephew Roger who had been proclaimed king in

1130. A new emperor, Manuel (1143–1180) had similar problems with their threatening presence. When the Turks captured Edessa in 1145, the Second Crusade was launched in outrage at the attack, and Roger of Sicily used it as a pretext to invade Corfu and Cephallonia in 1146 on his way to a destructive rampage through mainland Greece. Helped by the Venetians, Manuel briefly banished the Normans from the island. But by 1158, his attempts to recover the Italian states, through expansionist marriage alliances and peace treaties, united the Normans and Venetians against him. He was forced to make a peace treaty with Roger, and Cephallonia was handed back to the Normans yet again.

In 1185, any attempts at Byzantine rule on the island effectively ended. An alliance between William II, the ruler of Lower Italy and Sicily, and the Normans, led to the final dissolution of the Theme of Cephallonia, as they invaded Greece again. Margaritonis, a ruthless pirate and admiral of the Norman fleet, ransacked the island, massacring or taking hostage much of the populace. Count Margaritonis, as he now became, ruled over the newly formed Palatine Duchy of Cephallonia, Zakynthos and Lefkas. Sensibly, he made his headquarters at the fortress castle of Aghios Georgios instead of the old capital of Pale. His reign was short-lived. Escaping to the high seas and his old pirate ways, he was eventually captured and blinded, dying in captivity in Germany.

The beginning of Italian rule

In 1194, in the aftermath of the Third Crusade, which was sparked by Saladin's capturing Jerusalem from the Franks, Matteo Orsini, an even more colourful Italian pirate, established another reign of terror on the island when he seized Cephallonia, Zakynthos and Itháki under the guise

Opposite:
The ruins of the Castle of St George, the island capital between 1500 and 1759, with its commanding view over the Livatho plain towards Argostoli

of the Frankish flag. His was a dynasty that was to last until 1357. The year 1194 marked the end of Norman rule, and the beginning of the long reign of Italian families over the County Palatine of Cephallonia, including Zakynthos and Itháki, which lasted until 1483.

When the Crusaders sacked Constantinople in 1204, the Byzantine Empire was effectively divided up between the Franks and the Venetians. The Ionian islands supposedly came into Venetian hands when Matteo Orsini acknowledged their sovereignty. The reality was different as Orsini continued his own pirate activities, even co-operating with another notorious pirate, Leo Vetrano of Genoa, who was aligned to Norman Sicily. Coming under Papal scrutiny, Orsini was forced to cede the island to Pope Innocent III, although he continued to exercise power, becoming wealthier from his activities. The Vatican was not fooled. In 1207, Pope Innocent III abolished the orthodox religion and established Roman Catholicism on the island. Two years later, Orsini decided that Venice might be a more suitable ally, although he placated the Vatican's anger with a sizeable annual tribute to their burgeoning coffers.

The Orsini dynasty was characterized by endless subterfuge and ruthless murders, power-broking marriages and alliances amongst the Greek mainland nobility. Anything that seemed legitimate, and absolutely everything illegitimate, was attempted during their reign in order to ensure their hold over the island. On the eastern front, Matteo Orsini married his son Riccardo to the daughter of the last despot of Epirus, Thomas Comnenus, before declaring allegiance with the more powerful Villehardouins of the eparchy of Achaea.

Orsini died in 1303 and was succeeded by his son, John I, who became Count of Cephallonia. It would be hard to find a more

Left:
One of the Civil War's ELAS (National Popular Liberation Army) captains sits in a *kafeneion* **in Kouvalata village**

murderous, ambitious set of brothers than John's children, Nicholas and John II. Nicholas killed Thomas Comnenus and usurped the Epirot throne. He was murdered in his turn by his brother, John II, who proceeded to marry the Byzantine Emperor's daughter, Anna Palailogos. John II converted to the orthodox faith and changed his name to John Angelos Comnenus, only to be poisoned by his ambitious wife in 1335. The Orsini line died out and the island fell under the rule of King Philip I of Naples. In 1357, Philip's son Robert gave the island to three brothers, Leonardo, Pietro and Luigi de Tocchi, as a reward for saving his life in Germany.

The Tocchi family ruled successfully over Cephallonia until 1479, bringing some stability and respite from constant war. They were able to juggle the power struggles between various Italian states and Turkey without devastating the island too much. Outwardly, Cephallonia's recorded 40,000 inhabitants seemed relatively wealthy, at the very least they were well fed during this period. Leonardo I, who married Robert's sister Francesca, was the first 'Duke of Lefkada, Count of Cephallonia and Master of Vonitza'. Said to be a just ruler, he made some attempts to improve the impoverished islanders' day-to-day existence. His successor, Carlos I, made a marriage alliance with the Duchy of Athens, and thus expanded his empire into the mainland, helping to lessen the tax tributes paid by the islanders to

Right:
The interior of the Café Caruso in the small village of Komitata

Opposite:

Laying nets in the

early evening

other powerful Greek states, such as the eparchy of Achaea. When he died in 1429, he was succeeded by his nephew, Carlos II, who ruled until 1448 when he was succeeded by his young son, Leonardo III.

Leonardo allied himself to Venice, in a bid to strengthen his position in the battle against the Turks who were now controlling much of Epirus and Zakynthos. He moved his headquarters from Lefkada to Cephallonia's stronghold, the Castle of Aghios Georgios, and in the 1460s, probably trying to sway the local populace in his favour, he reintroduced the ortho-dox religion, without causing any major schisms with the Roman Catholic Church. After the fall of Constantinople to the Turks in 1453, the Venetians, together with Leonardo, were forced into an oppressive peace treaty with the Turks. When Leonardo refused to pay their heavy taxes, they became even more of a threat. The first war between Venice and Turkey broke out in 1463. When the Turks finally arrived on the island in 1479, under Ahmed, the pasha of Avlona, Leonardo was killed, leaving only his brother Antonio to try and save the island. It was a futile attempt and Antonio was also slaughtered, along with his supporters.

The Venetians had to pay further tribute to the Turks in order to be allowed to use shipping routes in the area. However, Turkish rule of the island of Cephallonia lasted less than twenty years. This was a miracu-lously short period of time, compared to the situation in the rest of Greece, where – except in certain Venetian colonies – Ottoman rule predominated between 1453 and 1800. Installed in the Castle of Aghios Georgios, the Turkish garrison was notoriously cruel, and many islanders fled, reducing the population to a mere 10,000 people.

Desperate to wrestle the island back from the Turks, the Venetians tried unsuccessfully to oust them from the Castle of Aghios Georgios in 1499, at the start of the second war between Venice and Turkey. In 1500, when Spain's 'Gran Capitan', Gonzalo Fernandez of Cordoba, called at the island to load timber from Mount Aenos, they enlisted his help. After a two-month siege of the castle, the Venetians, assisted by the Spanish troops, massacred the Turkish garrison. In a treaty with Sultan Beyazit II, at the end of the second war in 1504, the island finally passed into Venetian hands.

Cephallonia remained part of the Venetian Empire until 1797. Although in the sixteenth century it was plagued by constant attacks from pirate leaders of the Turkish fleet, such as the notorious Barbarossa and his followers, there was only one occasion when the Turks successfully stormed the island again. In 1538, a year after Suleiman the Magnificent declared war on Venice, the Turks laid waste to the island, and this time they were even more rapacious, taking 13,000 prisoners into a life of slavery. Remarkably, about 8,000 of those who were abducted eventually managed to return home. The war of 1570–74 between Turkey and Venice saw another brief attack on Sami but the Turks did not even bother to attempt to storm the impregnable Castle of Aghios Georgios.

After the fall of Cyprus in 1570, the Christian Armada amassed by the Pope, which had failed to reach the island in time, engaged the Turkish fleet in the Gulf of Corinth at Lepanto (modern-day Návpaktos) where there was a Venetian fortress. At the decisive Battle of Lepanto in 1571, the combined Venetian, Spanish and Genovese forces under Don John of Austria, the twenty-five-year-old son of the Holy Roman Emperor Charles V, defeated the Turks. Don John amassed his fleet in Sami, and many powerful Cephallonian families participated by sending galleys to this crucial battle that ended the Turkish threat to the West.

Opposite:
A view of Assos from its Venetian fortress, built in 1593

Cephallonia under the Venetians

During the long Venetian reign, the island once again proved to be of great strategic importance. Venice's military and commercial fleets used its abundant natural harbours as a vital staging post on the voyage to the colony of Crete and other Aegean islands. To counteract pirate raids, another fortress was built at Assos in 1593, as well as watch-towers along the island's long coastline. Cephallonia alone had a fleet of over 200 large and 4,000 small merchant ships plying their trade around the Mediterranean.

Life under the Venetians was highly regimented and class-bound. The island was ruled by a 'provleptis', a governor who resided in the castle of Aghios Georgios. In all, forty-seven of these governors ruled during the period of the Venetian occupation, although all important matters of state were usually decided by the doges themselves in Venice. Ostensibly, only the island nobility, who were registered in the *libra d'oro* (golden book), and who also made up the Council of the Community, had a say in island affairs. But this supposedly democratic body of over 150 members was as unruly as any modern-day parliament. As with all the Venetian colonies, the ruling nobility, despite intermarriage with local families of note, were not always popular with the Greeks. They built ostentatious palaces on the island which were in stark contrast to the simple rural homes of the hard-working locals. And although the Venetians provided relative stability, encouraging agriculture and trade, they also imposed severe taxes which caused the peasants considerable hardship. When Venice conquered the island, it immediately imposed taxes on all agricultural produce, even unborn lambs.

The nobility grew rich from the trade in agricultural products, especially raisins. These were Cephallonia's most important crop and were loaded at the Argostoli docks for export around Europe, a trade which the Venetians encouraged. Smugglers based on the island throughout this period took advantage of trade embargoes during the various wars between Venice and Turkey to build up a healthy black market. In 1603, when warehouses were built by the merchants to house these exports, Argostoli also began to be settled, and by 1632 it had a sizeable population.

As Venetian records show, the island's population increased dramatically with the steady influx of refugees from other areas of the Empire. It grew from a mere 14,000 in 1548 to 60,000 by 1655 (over double the island's current population). These records offer some indication that all strata of island society improved their standards of living as the economy flourished. Whenever colonies fell to the Turks, such as Cyprus in 1570, Crete in 1669 and the Peloponnese in 1715, refugees flooded on to the island. Today, many place and family names on the island are of Cretan origin.

In the seventeenth century, the island was racked by civil wars and severe earthquakes. In 1636 an earthquake claimed 540 lives and caused great damage to ancient ruins and many Byzantine churches. Between 1640 and 1642, civil war raged between the nobility and peasant farmers. It was broken up by the Venetians who sent an envoy to arrest the rebel leaders. For the next twelve years, until 1654, frequent infighting occurred amongst the nobility. In 1658 just as the 'provleptis' was about to launch an attack on the Turks, who had made the neighbouring island of Lefkada a base for their attacks on the Ionian islands, a second violent earthquake shook Cephallonia, destroying the town of Lixouri and claiming over 350 lives.

The Cretan connection with Cephallonia was particularly strong at this time. Despite the fact that the islanders benefited from the Turkish blockade of Crete, which allowed their own fleet to trade more freely and profitably around the Mediterranean, many islanders also assisted the Cretans during the long-drawn-out twenty-five-year siege by the Turks of the castle of Chandax in Candia (modern-day Iráklion). During the last three years of the siege, Louis XIV of France sent forty-five ships and 7,000 men to assist the Swiss General Verdmüller and Venice's commander Francesco Morosini, who was later to gain fame for blowing up the Parthenon in 1687 during the siege of the Acropolis.

From Cephallonia, the Antipas, Anninos and Deladetsima families came with small forces. Angelos Deladetsima, with 150 men, was among the chosen few to defend the castle during its final death throes. But, even with such earnest help, the Venetian stand against the Turks was ultimately fruitless and Crete fell in 1669. Many noble Cretan families sought refuge on Cephallonia at this time. There are also

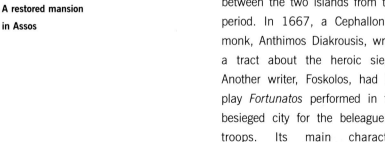

Right:
**A restored mansion
in Assos**

some interesting literary ties between the two islands from this period. In 1667, a Cephallonian monk, Anthimos Diakrousis, wrote a tract about the heroic siege. Another writer, Foskolos, had his play *Fortunatos* performed in the besieged city for the beleaguered troops. Its main character, Fortunatos, a Cephallonian soldier, ends up marrying a Cretan girl

called Petronella, a symbol of the popular ties forged between the two islands.

When Venice joined Austria in its war against the Turks in 1682, the Cephallonians assisted Francesco Morosini in capturing Lefkada and the Peloponnese in 1684. But, after the loss of the Peloponnese in 1715 – yet again to the Turks – the Venetian Empire went into rapid decline in Greece. Its last decades on the island were plagued by civil war and economic strife as the island nobility attempted to avoid paying the Republic's increasingly unfair taxes. Between 1755 and 1760, infighting between the powerful Aninos and Metaxas, Antipas and Karoussos, Typaldos and Loverdos families resulted in all the ringleaders being tried and hanged in Venice. In 1757 Argostoli became the island's capital and ten years later another earthquake claimed 253 lives.

One outcome of the long Venetian occupation was the gradual intellectual and cultural flowering of the island. Refugees from the Greek mainland and islands conquered by the Turks included painters and craftsmen who brought their own unique skills to Cephallonia. Children of the local nobility, educated in the best schools in Venice, Padua and Pisa, also brought back Western ideologies to the island. Compared to many of the Greek islands under the oppressive Ottoman yolk, Cephallonians enjoyed far greater artistic freedom that allowed them to develop a rich artistic heritage of their own. Some joined the increasing number of Greek intellectuals in exile in St Petersburg at the court of Catherine the Great or in Paris where they came under the heady influence of the French Revolution. Inspired by the writings of Voltaire, Rousseau and other French philosophers, intellectuals throughout Greece began to nurture hopes of independence for their own country.

Right:
Assos is one of the
island's prettiest
ports, filled with
waterfront
mansions and
tavernas

Right:
Olives being
processed at a local
olive mill

In the later half of the eighteenth century, as events unfolded in Europe, such as the French Revolution in 1789, Catherine the Great attempted to conquer the Ottoman Empire in the Balkans by taking various parts of the Peloponnese and the Aegean from the Turks. In 1792, she abandoned her ultimately unsuccessful expansionist plan.

French, Turkish and Russian rule

By now, the French had also begun to take an interest in Greece, establishing a consul in Ioannina where Ali Pasha, the Turkish governor of Epirus, had created a semi-autonomous state and looked greedily towards the nearby Ionian islands. In 1796, after Napoleon Bonaparte had conquered northern Italy, he sent an envoy to Ioannina in the first diplomatic attempts to gain control of the Ionian islands. In 1797, on 1 May, he declared war on Venice. There was great excitement when news reached Cephallonia that the French fleet had sailed into Corfu on 28 June 1797. Napoleon's representative, General Gentili, immediately issued a proclamation that French forces would liberate all the Ionian islands.

In Cephallonia, the islanders rejoiced in Argostoli by publicly burning the *libra d'oro* ('golden book'), flags of St Mark and lion coat-of-arms, all hated symbols of the Venetian republic's class-ridden autocratic rule. The infamous three-coloured French flag, symbolic of 'liberty, equality and fraternity' was hoisted in the main square, and a tree of liberty was planted and blessed by the archbishop. General Gentili noted in a letter not long afterwards: 'I am quite satisfied with the progress of equality in Cephallonia for they are all fine patriots.'

Opposite:
Olives are one of
the main island
crops

The 'Demarcheion', a democratic local government, was immediately set up in Argostoli, and schools and libraries were opened in an attempt to improve the island's lapsed educational standards among its large population. The last Venetian 'provleptis', James Marin, surrendered to the French, and Bonaparte accepted full sovereignty of the Ionian islands at the Treaty of Campo Formio on 17 October 1797. As for the acquisitive plans of Napoleon, he himself wrote that 'Corfu, Zante and Cephallonia are of more interest to us than all Italy.'

However, a year later, as Napoleon's invasion of Egypt brought him into direct conflict with the British, his ambitious drive eastwards was also causing the other great powers, Russia and Turkey, increasing concern. After his disastrous defeat by Lord Nelson at the Battle of Aboukir in 1798, the British agreed to Russia and Turkey taking control of the Ionian islands. In Cephallonia, the islanders now turned against the French, partly out of frustration at their continued economic strife, and also with the inevitable realization that the latest invaders were as bad as all the others. Skirmishes broke out in Lixouri and Livatho among the nobility and the peasants when the latter refused to recognize the hereditary rights of their landowners. The remaining French garrison was forced to flee the island for Corfu in September 1798. The Turkish-Russian fleet under Admiral Ushakov and Catir Bey liberated and restored order on the island yet again on 29 October 1798.

For the first time in their history, the islands were now to enjoy a strange kind of freedom and self-rule under the Turks and Russians. In the Treaty of Constantinople, signed on 21 March 1800, the United Septinsular Republic was born. Its first article set out the new regime:

His Majesty, the Emperor of all the Russias, considering that the said islands, formerly Venetian, on account of their proximity to the Morea

Opposite:
Aghia Evfimia on the east coast is a charming port, rebuilt after the 1953 earthquake to its original 1878 town plans with French funds

Left:
**At the northernmost
tip of the island,
Fiskardo is
surrounded by
beaches where
olive, pine and
cypress trees grow
down to the water's
edge**

and to Albania, particularly affect the security and tranquillity of the States of the Sublime Porte, it has been agreed, that the said islands shall form a Republic, subject, under title of Suzerainty, to the Sublime Porte, and governed by the principal and notable men of the country. His Imperial Majesty of all the Russias engages for himself and his successors to guarantee the integrity of the States of the said Republic, the maintenance of the Constitution which shall be accepted and ratified by the two high contracting powers, after having been submitted for their approbation, as well as the perpetuity of the privileges which shall be granted to them. His Majesty the Ottoman Emperor and his successors, being Suzerains of the said Republic, that is to say, Lords, Princes, and Protectors, and the said Republic being the vassal of the Sublime Porte, that is to say, dependent, subject, and protected, the duties of such protection shall be religiously observed by the Sublime Porte in favour of the said Republic.

Despite the obvious control by Russia and Turkey, it was still a political milestone for the cause of independence as the first self-governed state in Greece.

Although Russian forces remained on the islands until 1801, to protect them from the nearby threat of Ali Pasha, they now had their own flag and self-rule. But the government, composed solely of representatives of the nobility on each island, was bound to experience problems in the increasingly democratic and volatile climate. In Cephallonia, riots broke out in Lixouri, Argostoli and many of the island's villages. Particular animosity was felt between the occupants of Argostoli and Lixouri when the latter briefly became the capital of the island. On 23 December 1803,

Ioannis Mocenigo, a Zakynthian, was sent to restore law and order. A new constitution was drawn up that abolished all hereditary titles, allowed democratic elections, established Greek as the official language and even made the first known official recognition of a fledgling Greek nation.

By 1806, when war was declared on France by Austria, England, Russia and Prussia, it was inevitable that the Septinsular Republic would eventually become one of the jewels in the victor's crown. After defeating the allies at the battle of Austerlitz, Napoleon was ceded Russia's rights to the Ionian islands by Tsar Alexander II on 7 July 1807 at the Treaty of Tilsit. Napoleon immediately sent forces under General Berthier to occupy the islands again, with explicit orders to respect the islanders' autonomy. As the military governor, Berthier ignored Napoleon's request, preferring to rule with a corrupt iron hand. He was quickly replaced by General Donzelot who restored the more liberal 1803 constitution.

Despite some unrest, this final French occupation, lasting only two years, was warmly welcomed by the islanders until economic hardships began again. As part of Britain's continuing war against Napoleon, there was a general blockade of the Ionian islands. Vessels flying the French flag were seized and taken to Malta to be sold, and there was a shortage of vital foodstuffs such as wheat. Anti-French propaganda was also instigated by the pro-British nobility, many of whom had become agents actively promoting the British cause. Eventually, the Cephallonians sent a petition to the British in Malta, asking to be saved. By the time three British frigates with over 3,000 soldiers had sailed from Messina in Sicily, capturing the neighbouring island of Zakynthos on 2 October 1809, the Cephallonians were preparing themselves for their inevitable new rulers.

Opposite:
Wild flowers surround the fields and cliffs of the Assos peninsula

From British to Greek Rule

On 5 October 1809, the British took Cephallonia. Commanding the land and naval forces, Brigadier General Sir John Oswald and Captain Springer, RN met little resistance from the French as they sailed into Argostoli harbour. Most had either fled to Corfu or were holed up in the Castle of Aghios Georgios where Lorenzo Pieri, *chef de bataillon* of the French troops, swiftly surrendered. Itháki and Kythera were the next islands to be liberated, although it took another five years for Corfu to come into British hands. Lieutenant Colonel Hudson Lowe was made provisional head of the temporary British administration, which included a local government composed of Cephallonians.

The following year, in March, the British attacked nearby Santa Maura (modern-day Lefkada) which was still held by the French, who were encouraging Albanian rebels to attack the liberated islands. Major Charles-Philippe de Bosset, a Swiss serving in the British army, was sent from Messina with two companies to relieve Oswald's forces. After the island fell on 16 April, de Bosset immediately took over the command of Cephallonia as the provisional head of its government.

Improvements to the island under de Bosset

Joseph Partsch, a German historian and geographer, spent five years, from 1885, exploring the island extensively, making detailed maps. Noted for his book *Kephallenia und Ithaka, Eine geographische Monographie*, Partsch had this to say about the British invasion:

The end of the strife during 1809 saw the task of restoring this small neglected island fall to Britain. Law and order reigned from the very beginning of the British occupation. Turbulence throughout the island

Opposite:
A view of Fiskardo harbour

Opposite:
**Abandoned today,
the old town of
Skala was
completely
destroyed by the
1953 earthquake**

and a ruined economy demanded, as the only solution, drastic measures and the resolute firmness of a powerful and wise government. The first signs of creative activity became apparent when Major de Bosset, a Swiss from Neuchâtel serving in the British army, built the long bridge spanning the harbour of Argostoli. Although the British showed a marked preference for Corfu, yet more public works were carried out for the benefit of the wild and rocky island and its intractable inhabitants than for any of the other Ionian islands.

Right:
**Entrance to the
cemetery in the old
town of Skala
destroyed by the
1953 earthquake**

Over the next four years, de Bosset accomplished some impressive public enterprises that left the islanders amazed. He immediately set about building roads connecting Argostoli with Sami, Assos, Skala and the villages of Livatho, the most densely populated area of the island. Suddenly, remote areas became accessible and local trade flourished with the easier modes of transportation.

As immediate thanks, he was given a magnificent ceremonial sword by the Livatho village elders, with the acknowledgement:

Cephallonia experienced all the inconvenience attending a want of good roads and easy communication; existing roads were not only inconvenient but often impassable; the advancement of civilization, the internal commerce and agriculture of the island and the progress of travellers, were in consequence greatly impeded: your firmness and perseverance have removed these inconveniences by causing the construction of solid and spacious roads which will prove so many durable monuments to transmit your name to our descendants ... The inhabitants can no longer refrain from public manifestation of their heartfelt gratitude to you, and they accordingly request your acceptance of a sword, as a mark of their acknowledgement of the many advantages for which they are indebted to you.

Apart from involving almost every available islander in the flurry of road construction, de Bosset also began to improve the facilities in Argostoli town. One of the first things he did was to clean up its main street – known as the Lithostroto, after its Roman paving stones – which was extremely unhygienic. Illegal wooden balconies had been added to every building, and these blocked out any light and air on the street below; in addition, rubbish was constantly thrown from them. The street was filled with butchers' shops where animals were routinely slaughtered, and their blood allowed to run into the street. De Bosset had the balconies removed, the butchers' shops moved to another street and a slaughter-house built on the outskirts of town at Koutavos Bay. His next step was to install street lighting – forty lamps with wicks that burnt olive oil – around the town, and improve the squares in Argostoli and Lixouri.

By 1812 he was planning a bolder project – to build a bridge across isolated Argostoli's bay in order to connect it with the Trapano shoreline opposite. Previously, Argostoli had always been reached by boat when-ever occupants of inland villages had ventured to this area. But when the sea was too rough, they either had to wait until it improved or take the long, circuitous and often dangerous route around the muddy Koutavos marshes to reach the town. When de Bosset first proposed the idea to the local Cephallonian councillors, explaining how the bridge would aid communication and help develop trade, it was met with much scepti-cism. Writing in 1859, Marino Salomon described the scene:

Opposite:
In 1812, Major Charles-Philippe de Bosset, a Swiss officer serving in the British army, built the Trapano bridge, still standing today in Argostoli
Inset:
de Bosset did much for Cephallonia between 1809 and 1818 when he was in charge of the island under British rule

During the following session the majority voted against the plan under the pretext that the peasants from the adjacent villages of Dilinata, Faraclata, Omala and Pirgi had, in the past, invaded the city intent on looting, arson and carnage and carrying out their own vendettas. The construction of a bridge would lay open the town at all hours and seasons to incursions by such rustics.

Not convinced by their arguments, de Bosset apparently drew his sword and threw it on the table, saying, 'My sword shall cut the Gordian knot.'

Fifteen days later the Trapano bridge was built. Spanning over a quarter of a mile, its initial causeway was made of timber, later to be replaced by the permanency of solid stone, arched at regular intervals to allow water to flow into the lagoon that it created on one side. Of course, once the new bridge had been built, the inhabitants of Argostoli were delighted. Yet again, de Bosset was rewarded; this time with a gold medal and the following citation from the Executive Council of Cephallonia:

The bridge of Trapano, a project which had never before been formed and which, when conceived by him was considered by others to be impracticable, he undertook after mature deliberation and executed in a style that calls to memory the Greek mode of construction, without cement; this bridge in the wide harbour of Argostoli which it crosses, forms an ample fishery and at the same time places several of the most extensive and populous districts in immediate communication with the town.

Opposite:
The ruins of the village of Farsa where Louis de Bernières was inspired to write ***Captain Corelli's Mandolin***

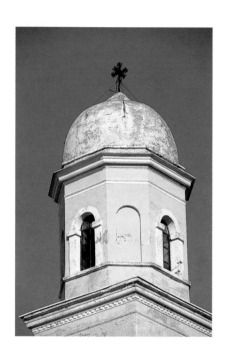

A year later, halfway across the bridge, de Bosset constructed a square with an obelisk in the middle, surrounded by twelve pillars that were connected by iron chains. The obelisk bore the simple inscription, in four languages (English, Latin, Italian and Greek): 'To the Glory of the British Nation by the Cephaloniots'. Thirty years later, when it had fallen into disrepair, the bridge was reconstructed and widened, with sixteen stone arches and a stone parapet to protect it from high waves and winds. This imposing construction still stands today, having withstood the 1953 earthquake – testimony to its fine construction.

De Bosset's greatest road was built in 1812, crossed Mount Evmorfia and connected Argostoli with Sami and the fertile valleys on the east coast. Lord Henry Holland expressed his admiration for the road in his book *Travels in the Ionian Islands and Albania in 1812 and 1813*.

The road beginning from the new causeway at Argostoli, and traversing the mountains in the centre of the isle, to the opposite coast near Samos, is the greatest undertaking of its kind. It had been executed when I was in Cefalonia, so far as to be everywhere perfectly passable for a carriage, and the journey from Argostoli to this coast, which formerly required eight or ten hours, might now be performed in little more than half the time. The road carried along the populous district of the southern coast might also be compared with those of England, and is greatly superior to any I have seen in Portugal or Sicily.

During the course of his road building, de Bosset also indulged in some amateur archaeology, exploring the ancient cities of Krane, Same, Pale and Pronoi, and excavating amongst the Mycenaean rock tombs at

Left:
The church at Messovounia, one of the inland villages of the Erissos region

Mazarakata, near Metaxata. He also unearthed the foundations and statues at an ancient temple near Skala on the east coast. This small Doric temple at Gradou was his favourite discovery, probably because he was the first person seriously to excavate at the site.

In 1815 de Bosset was recalled to Corfu by Sir Thomas Maitland, the new Resident of the Lord High Commissioner of the Ionian islands. On 22 March 1818, Lieutenant General Sir John Oswald wrote to de Bosset, who was now commanding the Parga territories:

I at various times witnessed with admiration, the change you effected in the physical appearance and convenience of the island, and in the moral conduct and habits of the population. I certainly left you there with the deep impression that by appointing you chief of the local government of Cephallonia I had conferred a great blessing on its inhabitants. I have ever held this opinion, and it has uniformly afforded me the highest satisfaction to express these sentiments to his Royal Highness the Commander-in-Chief, and to such of his Majesty's ministers as are more particularly connected with the interests of the Ionian islands.

De Bosset retired in 1820, settling in his house in Rue du Musée in Neuchâtel, surrounded by forty-eight Mycenaean vases from Mazakarata, which he later donated to a local museum.

Corfu was finally wrestled from the French in 1814. After Napoleon's defeat, Britain, Russia, Austria and Prussia met at the Congress of Vienna to discuss the fate of the Ionian islands. On 5 November 1815, the Duke of Wellington, Lord Castlereagh, Capodistria and Prince de Rasoumoffsky signed the Treaty of Paris under which the 'United States of the Ionian

Left:
Halfway across the
Trapano bridge, de
Bosset constructed
a square with an
obelisk in the
middle, surrounded
by 12 pillars that
were connected by
iron chains, with
the simple
inscription in
4 languages:
(English, Latin,
Italian and Greek):
'To the Glory of the
British Nation by
the Cephalloniots'.
Inset:
The obelisk as it
stands today

62

islands' were formally made a British protectorate. Article VII of the Treaty sets out some of the terms:

The trading flag of the United States of the Ionian islands shall be acknowledged by all the contracting parties as the flag of a free and independent state. It shall carry with the colours, and above the armorial bearings thereon displayed before the year of 1807, such other as his Britannic Majesty may think proper to grant, as a mark of the protection under which the said Ionian States are placed; and for the more effectual furtherance of this protection, all the ports and harbours of the said States are hereby declared to be, with respect to the honorary and military rights, within British jurisdiction.

Based in Corfu, the first British Lord High Commissioner of the Ionian islands was the unpopular and autocratic ruler Sir Thomas Maitland. His controversial 1817 constitution concentrated almost all power in his hands, with as little as possible given over to the local legislative assembly. When Parga on the mainland was handed over to the Turks in 1819, in actual compliance with the 1815 Treaty, Maitland bore all the blame for what was widely seen by the Greeks as a betrayal of their dream of an eventual independent state. Henry Jervis White, in his book *History of the Island of Corfu and of the Republic of the Ionian Islands*, says of him, 'Few men have had more enemies, or more scurrilous abuse.' Maitland died in Malta in 1824 of an apoplectic stroke. He was succeeded by Sir Frederic Adam who governed until 1831. An altogether more liberal commissioner, Adam took an interest in education, and established the Ionian Academy in Corfu.

Charles James Napier

If de Bosset was admired by the islanders, Charles James Napier was positively worshipped. He is still remembered today on the island, even if many of his physical accomplishments have been destroyed. This forty-two-year-old hero of the Peninsular War took up his appointment as Resident of the Lord High Commissioner on Cephallonia on 12 March 1822. For the next nine years, until 1830, in the best philanthropic colonial tradition, Napier worked tirelessly to improve the island by building more roads, bridges, public buildings and parks. He also granted loans to farmers to help them increase their crops, and attempted to establish free access to all the island's eight ports (especially Assos) to aid trade, although this was in fact denied by the High Commissioner.

Later in his life he reminisced:

Being, however, resolved to do my best, I went to work with the hopes of supplying my defects by zeal and industry. I trusted that a knowledge of details would come naturally, in tracing evil results, to their causes, and why Cephallonia should not be a rich and powerful island ... That I remedied these evils wholly, I will not say, all I can assert is that I saw them, and remedied them as far as my abilities.

He soon became a passionate philhellene, so incensed that he could not assist the Greeks more during the War of Independence when they were defeated at Missolonghi in 1826, that he wrote in anguish: 'Letters from the chiefs in Missolonghi turning to me for help which they will not believe I have no power to give them! This is dreadful to me – would to God I could do anything to save them even at the expense of my own life

Left:
Portrait of Charles James Napier, the island's most popular Resident of the Lord High Commissioner between 1822 and 1830

Opposite:
A fishing boat at Sami

Left:
**Old fashioned
larders in a
shepherds hut**

– the poor Suliots think me General, Admiral, everything! Are all those gallant men to die – Good God!' He also learned modern Greek from a scholar priest by the name of Neofytos Vamvas, and perhaps coaxed by his friendship with Lord Byron who also stayed on the island, he became a genuine devotee of the rugged charms of its landscape and inhabitants.

As P. Vergotis notes in the Greek journal *Parnassos* in 1893: 'He had a great sense of humour and, although he could be very violent when roused by injustice, he was basically tender-hearted towards women and children and the suffering.' Returning from a private visit to London in 1825, Napier recorded in his diary: 'Now I am once more amongst the merry Greeks, who are worth all other nations together. I like to see them, I like to hear them; I like their fun, their good humour, their paddy ways, for they are very like Irishmen. All their bad habits are Venetian; their wit, their eloquence, their good nature are their own.'

Napier's greatest legacy was to instigate some genuinely utilitarian public buildings and the remarkable modern network of roads and bridges around the previously inaccessible island. All the bridges survived the 1953 earthquake, except the Drakata bridge which had been blown up in 1943 by Italian troops trying to hinder the German invasion. One of his first acts was to ask for the help of an army engineer, John Pitt Kennedy, who had previously completed major work on Lefkada's harbour before returning home to Ireland. Aged twenty-six, Kennedy became Director of Public Works and Military Secretary to the Resident between 1822 and 1832, refusing the offer of a job as Governor of Australia in 1831. He was indispensable to Napier, as the latter records in his diary: 'Captain John Kennedy, the island secretary, completely entered into my views, and by his honesty, ability and activity enabled me to accomplish more than double what either of us could have done singly.'

The two became lifelong friends, as their letters to each other when overseas reveal. For example, on 28 November 1828, Kennedy wrote to Napier in London:

My Dear Colonel,
I have received your two letters dated Corfu, together with the socks and
smoothing irons, and Piggy's [Napier's daughter Susan who was left on
the island.] toes return you warm thanks for your present. I have been
frequently at Racli and things go on smoothly but slow in consequence
of the weather. It has been one continued torrent of rain this whole
month.

During the 1820s, all the 134 miles of roads on the island were constructed using the corvée system ('angaria' in Greek), whereby every islander – and, on Napier's orders, every Englishman – was required to work, unpaid, one day every fortnight on the roads. The whole island was opened up by this new network. Those who didn't want to work had to pay an amount of money towards the building costs, the amount calculated according to their means. And it seems that most were happy to pay, either in cash or with their labour. As Napier records in 1822: 'No man but a pauper is exempt from its operation: nobles, priests, peasants, all work or pay according to their means ... Four years' work ought to be sufficient to complete the roads if the Corvée is vigorously enforced: as it is not, I should say it will require eight.'

Napier applied the Scotsman John Loudon MacAdam's system of road-making using broken stone, which had been widespread in Great

Right:
A picture of
Argostoli before the
1953 earthquake
destroyed the town
Inset:
A portrait of the
grandfather of
Alexandros
Kavallieratos

Britain since 1815 when MacAdam had been appointed a surveyor general of roads in Bristol. There were plenty of local materials to utilize: "The materials which abound in Cephallonia for making roads, are hard and soft limestone and red earth, which, when mixed, form a cement. The *Tuffo* or soft limestone is of a brown sand colour, very porous and when first exposed to the air, is cut with hatchets, like Malta stone, and is soon pounded and trod into a solid mass when laid on the roads.'

Writing to his mother on 10 June 1822, Napier says: 'Health besets me. Up early and writing till eight; then feed and work in office till twelve, sometimes till three o'clock; swim, dine and then horseback visiting the road making ... expect no letters from me save about roads. My head is so full of them that I think more of MacAdam than of anything else.'

An example of Napier's road-building skills can still be seen today between Agrapidies and Mount Roudi on the way to Sami. No longer in use, this 3-kilometre stretch remains in good condition and demonstrates the stone-cutting skills of the British army and locals. Napier was justifiably proud: 'My Samos road is beautiful, I hardly ever saw anything so magnificent as the scenery except in the Tyrol.'

But this was only the beginning of Napier and Kennedy's outstanding teamwork. Between them, they designed and executed a remarkable number of buildings in less than a decade; never extravagantly, and always resourcefully, given the difficulty and delay they experienced in obtaining funds from the Lord High Commissioner in Corfu. Two new lighthouses were erected, one on Vardiani island and one at the entrance of the harbour at the point of Aghios Theodori. This round, elegant building, encircled by Doric columns, was destroyed in the 1875 earthquake, and subsequently restored to its original plans. Today, it is a favourite spot from which to view the sunset. They also demolished the old Venetian Quarantine station just outside the harbour, building a new one together with a barracks, health office and hospital that became known as the Lazaretto. A new prison, based on some of the enlightened principles of Jeremiah Bentham's prison reforms, offered more humane conditions to its inmates. Both were destroyed in the 1953 earthquake.

Argostoli and Lixouri also both benefited from new streets and harbour quays, making them both cleaner and more attractive for the local inhabitants. Argostoli was the first to be tackled by Napier: 'The town of Argostoli had a ragged, filthy edge, and generally shallow water. In strong winds, the waves dashed into the town, so as to render the street next to the sea impassable; I therefore resolved to build a quay.' Unfortunately, Napier removed stones from the Roman Agora remains (next to the ancient city of Krane), to construct the 1½-kilometre long quay.

After a market was built in Argostoli, it was time to reward Lixouri with an even finer construction, the Markato, unfortunately also destroyed in the 1953 earthquake. Using stone quarried at Fallari on Mount Aenos, Kennedy drew up the architectural plans for the colonnaded neo-classical building which housed market and law courts, a large main hall seating 600 people and a school.

During part of the construction, Kennedy wrote to Napier who was in England: 'We have got the five columns, and as soon as I get one more which will complete one end, "I shall rest on my oars" until I see how the money goes and get it covered as it would not do to make a dandy market of it, all ruffles and no shirt.' Eight thousand people attended the inauguration of this building, applauding the two men as they landed by boat from Argostoli, for an opening party in Lixouri's main square just in front of the Markato.

At this time, Napier also observed the traditional rivalry between the two towns: 'There is a mortal hatred between the inhabitants of Argostoli and Lixouri. The former were therefore jealous of the beautiful structure which they beheld arise in the rival town; I wished to support Lixouri. I am sure that two handsome small towns are better for the people than one large one, being more clean, more healthy and more moral.'

Another egalitarian project was a model farm at Pronnus, near Poros on the east coast, where a small colony of Maltese settlers was started with twenty-seven families and a total of 278 people. It housed Maltese stone-workers and their families, imported for their construction skills, and was eventually disbanded because most of the workers were found to be either sick with malaria or involved in smuggling activities.

All this activity appears even more remarkable when you consider the political and social upheavals that were occurring in the 1820s. At first starvation was widespread in the northern part of the island because of the lack of roads and the closure of the Fiskardo and Assos ports. Then, on 25 March 1821, the Greek flag was raised by Philiki Etairia, the Greek secret society that was the founder of the independence movement, thus beginning the Greek struggle for independence. During this struggle, the

Right:
An old view of
Argostoli harbour

73

Left:
**The shutters of
an island house
in Assos**

British authorities were unwilling openly to assist the rebels, because of their diplomatic obligations under the 1800 Treaty of Constantinople with the Turks, and because, through the Treaty of Paris, they had just ceded Parga to the dangerous, widely hated Ali Pasha.

Many prominent Cephallonians were members of Philiki Etairia, when it started the first uprisings in the Peloponnese. They worked secretly on the island, and more openly abroad, to spread the word about the cause. Cephallonian fighting units also played a crucial role in defeating the Turks at the Battle of Lala in northern Epirus in 1821.

In 1826, refugees flooded on to the island during the fall of Missolonghi on the mainland. There were frequent letters from British officers to the powerless Napier. One, from George Jarvis, records the desperate state to which the remaining inhabitants were reduced:

I beg you colonel to send us immediately either from Cephallonia or Zante a man of war or such transport as you can, to render these last services to the garrison of Missolonghi which are due to patriotic valour ... There is no alternative left; a few days ago the Turks have again been repulsed with a great loss but the Greeks are six days without bread and had already slaughtered their horses and cats.

In 1830, Napier left the island with his wife Elizabeth who was gravely ill. They left their two daughters in the care of the Reverend Dixon and his wife at the Monastery of Aghiou Apostolou Andrea in Peratata. Elizabeth died soon after their arrival and Napier also learned of the annulment of his job by Sir Frederick Adam. Kennedy wrote often to his friend before he himself left for Ireland in 1831.

Neither man ever returned to Cephallonia but they did meet again in India ten years later. Appointed Commander-in-Chief, on behalf of the East India Company, in 1841, General Sir Charles Napier immediately offered the post of Military Secretary to Kennedy. Like Cephallonia before her, the greatest British colony also benefited from the considerable energies and skills of the two men who built more roads and railways around its dusty plains and hills.

D.T. Ansted, who wrote about the island in 1863 in his book *The Ionian Islands*, adds this suitable epitaph:

He has the credit of having originated all useful measures, and there can be no doubt that his energy and great talent were fully exercised during his government of the island. That he ruled with a rod of iron, acknowledging no law but that which seemed to him good for the occasion; that he went about armed with a walking-stick, which he freely used on the backs of those who offended him, though probably never without reason; all these anomalies were rather reasons for popularity than the contrary with a people like the Greeks, and at a time like that during which he was chief. The anecdotes about him are very numerous, and all smack of the same peculiarity. He was a tyrant, but he was strictly just, even against himself as well as against all evil doers. He insisted on every one about him doing his will, but his will rarely exceeded that which ought also to have been the desire and intention of every one. Of all things road-making seems to have been his hobby, and his chief employment while in the island. Quarrelling with the High Commissioner was an amusing relaxation he allowed himself in large measure. The road-making, however, he attended to thoroughly and unceasingly.

Opposite:
A view of the port of Poros on the east coast

In the 1830s, whilst the fledgling country of modern Greece began life as a monarchy under King Otto, there was a more liberal period of rule on the island. After Lord Nugent became High Commissioner in 1831, more political reforms were granted, such as freedom of the press and increased power for the local parliamentary representatives. The next Commissioner, Baron Howard Douglas (1834–41) was not as popular. The subsequent Commissioners, Alexander MacKenzie (1841–43) and Lord John Seaton (1843–49), had an easier time on the island with their liberal administrations. Under MacKenzie, Charles Seabright, Baron d'Everton, was appointed Resident of the island in 1842. He managed to find funds to reconstruct Napier's roads, which had all fallen into disrepair, and he also drained the marshes at Sami and improved its port facilities.

Political turmoil on the island

But in 1848, the year of revolutions throughout Europe, political turmoil was about to break out again when Cephallonia responded with its own uprisings. The first, known as the Stavros revolt, erupted on 14 September when 200 islanders marched on Argostoli. They were stopped on the Trapano bridge by British troops. Arriving from Corfu, the Commissioner, Lord John Seaton, was forced to grant an amnesty to the ringleaders, freedom to hold meetings and form political parties. Three parties were formed soon afterwards: the Rizospastic, or Radical, party whose main aim was 'Enosis' (union) of the Ionian islands with Greece; the Reformist party who proclaimed that it was too early for such dreams and campaigned for further reforms to the 1817 constitution; and the Conservative party (nicknamed 'the fiends') which aligned itself with the British and favoured a continuance of their rule.

Opposite:
A small fishing boat in Assos harbour

The second uprising, the Skala revolt, broke out on 15 August 1849. This time the uprising was inspired by land-owning members of the Conservative party. They were worried that they were going to lose some of their privileges when the Ionian Parliament declared that Queen Victoria was prepared to ratify some more suggested reforms of the 1817 constitution. The uprising was quelled in a much bloodier manner than the previous one and the twenty-one ringleaders were all hanged, thirty-four others were jailed and eighty-seven whipped. Other party leaders were exiled.

In 1850, the British Parliament approved the constitutional reforms. The first free elections were held, returning ten representatives to the 'Ninth Ionian Parliament'. The Radical party won the election. When Yannis Typaldos, one of its MPs, attempted to read out a proclamation on 26 November, asking, on behalf of all the inhabitants of the Ionian islands, for 'Enosis', all parliamentary proceedings were suspended by the Speaker on orders of the High Commissioner. In 1851, all parliamentary parties were banned on Cephallonia and yet more of their leaders were arrested and exiled.

By 1855, the calls for unification were becoming more widespread throughout the islands. A more moderate Commissioner, John Young, was appointed who tried to placate the populace by allowing the Radicals to return to the Ionian Parliament in 1857. In 1858 William Gladstone was sent as High Commissioner Extraordinary, in an attempt by the British Government to sort out the grievances of the Ionian islands. On his tour of the islands he was greeted everywhere by the call for 'Enosis' but could only recommend further constitutional changes. He told the House of Commons, in 1861, that such a course of action (i.e. union)

would be 'nothing less than a crime against the peace of Europe'.

Despite this claim, events in Greece forced the British Government's hand, after King Otto abdicated in 1862 following uprisings against him. With Britain's approval, Prince William George, the second son of the King of Denmark, was proclaimed the next King of the Hellenes on 30 March 1863. A new constitution meant that Greece also became a real democracy on paper for the first time – a *'vasilivomeni dimokratia'* (democracy under a King) with its own *vouli* (Parliament). At the same time, despite Gladstone's remarks, the Ionian islands were finally ceded to Greece. At a treaty signed in London (The London Protocol) the 13th Ionian Parliament declared on 23 September 1863: 'The islands, Corfu, Cephallonia, Zakynthos, Lefkas, Ithaka, Kythira, Paxi and the other small islands are united with the Kingdom of Greece in order to be its part for ever, unseparable, in one and only state, under the constitutional sceptre of his Majesty the King of Greece, George I and his successors.'

The last Ionian Parliament was formally dissolved on 7 April 1864. On 21 May 1864 the official ceremony took place to hand over the islands to a Greek envoy. A month later, King George I visited the islands. For Cephallonia's population of 74,000 it was a time to rejoice as they finally became part of the Greek kingdom. As D.T. Ansted had noted a year earlier: 'Let not an apparent failure or early troubles discourage those who wish well to Greece. The way to freedom is not smooth and flowery. Freedom loves to dwell on rocky shores and in almost inaccessible haunts; but Greece has already been her home, and she does not easily forget the spots once made sacred by her presence.'

The emerging state of Greece

From the late nineteenth century onwards, as the Greek kingdom extended its territories, Cephallonia's history inevitably becomes entwined with the emerging state of modern Greece. Every island and mountain town and village throughout the new kingdom could not fail to be affected by the immense economic and political problems and debates of the fledgling state.

Thessaly was annexed in 1881. During the two Balkan wars of 1912–13 and 1917–18, when Greece finally and briefly entered the First World War, territorial gains were even more substantial, including Macedonia, southern Epirus, Crete and Samos. After the First World War, when the Great Powers met at the Treaty of Sèvres in 1920, other areas of the Ottoman Empire were carved up, raising Greek nationalist hopes even further when the country was promised Thrace, the Gallipoli peninsula, parts of the Marmora Sea and the northern Aegean islands of Imbros and Tenedos, close to the Turkish coast.

The treaty was never ratified, leading Greece into the disastrous consequences of the 'Great Idea', whereby they attempted to take Constantinople, and expand the 'Empire' to include some of the boundaries it once held in ancient times. This led to the catastrophic exchange of populations in 1922 – with the expulsion of over one and a half million Greeks from Asia Minor, especially the Greek city of Smyrna (modern-day Izmir) and a far smaller number of Turks from Thrace.

One effect of this huge influx of refugees, apart from the difficulty of assimilating them into a country with already weakened infrastructures caused by incessant Balkan wars, was the subtle cultural and political changes to the country's make-up as these more cosmopolitan Greeks

Opposite:

Pilgrims come from all over Greece to visit the monastery of Aghios Gerasimos at Omala where the island's patron saint, Aghios Gerasimos's remains are kept. He was so popular that he has two annual feast days, on 16 August and 20 October

settled in towns and cities all over Greece. Greek Communism began to take a hold at this time, inspired by the new working-class masses and the Russian Revolution, and many party members were Asia Minor Greeks. From the late nineteenth century until the mid twentieth century, Cephallonia, like other parts of Greece, was also plagued by large-scale emigration to the New World, especially to Australia and to North and South America.

Wars and natural disasters

One of Greece's most famous twentieth-century politicians was also a Cephallonian. Educated in Germany, Ioannis Metaxas first came to prominence in 1915 when, as Chief of the General Staff, he advised King Constantine I not to take sides against Germany, Austria and Turkey. He was a monarchist but also staunchly pro-Greek. In 1923, with fascism taking hold in Europe, and Mussolini having seized power in Italy in 1922, General Metaxas also attempted an unsuccessful *coup d'état*. By 1936 he was prime minister and, as Germany and Italy threatened European stability, George II, the new King of Greece, came to rely more and more on Metaxas, granting him the right to govern by decree.

Metaxas used these powers to ban trade unions and strikes, and arrest Communist leaders. Bloodshed followed and Parliament was dissolved. Metaxas now emerged as fascist dictator of Greece, ruling until his death in January 1941. He is remembered today chiefly as the man who notoriously said 'No' in a telegram to Mussolini on 28 October 1940. This was the day, still celebrated as a public holiday in Greece, when he replied to Mussolini's ultimatum following the fabricated Albanian border incidents that attempted to incriminate Greece and provoke the country

Opposite:
A view of Sami

Το Βρετανικό αντιτορπιλικό "ΝΤΕΡΙΝ" ήταν το πρώτο πλοίο που με κυβερνήτη τον Πλοίαρχο Πέρσυ Γκικ πρός την 13 Αυγούστου 1953 στο κατεστραμμένο από τον φοβερό σεισμό της προηγούμενης Αργοστόλι καί προσέφερε τις πρώτες βοήθειες. Η ΚΕΦΑΛΟΝΙΑ θυμάται.

H.M.S. "DARING" was the first ship under the command of captain Percy Gick R.N. to arrive in Argostoli on the 13th of August 1953 and offer help. A devastating earthquake destroyed the town the previous day. KEFALONIA remembers

Left:
The gates to the British cemetery at Argostoli
Inset:
the plaque commemorating HMS Daring's assistance in rebuilding and helping the inhabitants of Argostoli immediately after the 1953 earthquake

Right:
**A wartime mine is
used to collect
rainwater by this
couple in Skala**

into war. The Greeks became the only nation voluntarily to join the British in their fight against Germany and the Axis powers. Metaxas died shortly afterwards and, on 5 April 1941, the Germans began their attack on Greece, which ended swiftly in May when they took Crete.

The Germans released most of the imprisoned Communist leaders, who immediately set about organizing a resistance movement. Their cause was helped by problems during the German Occupation, such as a series of puppet governments, a powerless government in exile in Egypt, and starvation among the population, brought about by the severity of Allied blockades. Such miseries swelled the numbers of willing resistance fighters. Four rival organizations, EAM (National Liberation Front), ELAS (National Popular Liberation Army), EDES (National Republican Greek League) and EKKA (National and Social Liberation), jostled for power, each with differing political aims, apart from the obvious common one of the removal of German forces. As the German forces withdrew in May 1945, these factions continued to fight for power in the aftermath of the Second World War.

The bitter Civil War of 1946–49 that followed caused even further divisions within the Greek nation; instead of the hoped-for economic and social reconstruction that was occurring in the rest of Europe, for the Greeks there were yet more deprivations and degradations.

Three events in the twentieth century have irrevocably scarred

Cephallonia's psyche: the massacre of occupying Italian forces on the island at the end of the Second World War; the devastating earthquake of 1953; and the tourism of the past few decades, which has brought both new-found wealth and the all-too-common ugliness of hastily built resort hotels and guest-houses. The former two events are movingly described in fictional form in Louis de Bernières' best-selling novel *Captain Corelli's Mandolin*.

The Italians invaded the island in April 1941. The occupation was relatively harmonious until the Armistice between Italy's Badoglio Government in Brindisi and the Allies at the beginning of September 1943. German troops, under Colonel Barge, anticipating this new situation, had already started to invade and occupy the island in August. General Gandin, the commander of the Italian Army's Alpine 'Acqui' Division, which was already on the island, hesitated over whether to surrender to the Germans on the orders of *Supergreccia* (the Italian Command in Greece), or to obey Badoglio's orders to resist the Germans. The result of his indecision was the tragedy of the 'Cephallonian Martyrs'.

Most of the 9,000 Italian troops refused to surrender, preferring to resist the Germans, and aided by some EAM resistance fighters, they fought for nine bloody days between 15 and 26 September, in an abortive attempt to stop the Germans, who had by this time been reinforced by two battalions of the German Alpine division under Major von Hirchfeld, with air support from Stukka and Messerschmitt fighter planes. The real tragedy was that the superior numbers of Italian troops could easily have defeated the 3,000 troops of the 996th regiment which were all that Colonel Barge had at his disposal at the time of the Armistice.

On surrendering to the Germans, the Italians were all massacred on

Opposite:
Aghios Gerasimos's feast day on 20 October

Left:
**Saint Gerasimos's
remains are carried
in a silver cask
during the
procession on
20 October**

Hitler's personal orders. Most of the 341 officers and 4,750 soldiers were herded into trucks and taken to the 'Casetta Rossa' ('Red Villa') and surrounding hills close to the Aghios Theodori lighthouse to be slaughtered. All over the island where massacres took place, the bodies were burned to try and hide the evidence of this futile action, and hastily buried in mass graves or thrown into the sea. Only thirty-four survived the carnage by shamming death amongst the bodies of their comrades. Some claim the number of dead to be much higher.

Survivors wrote moving testaments of their experiences, such as the 'Acqui' Division's chaplain, Padre Luigi Ghilardini, in his book *I Martiri di Cefalonia*. Today, there is a well-kept Italian cemetery on a hill, above Aghios Theodori, with plaques and a small chapel to the 'Martyrs', although most of the bodies were removed in 1953 to be buried in Bari. Afterwards, the German occupation of the island lasted less than a year. They retreated on 10 September, covering their tracks by making sure that every body and every piece of evidence was burned or buried. Only the eyewitness accounts of horrified islanders and survivors remain.

The other traumatic event on the island was the 1953 earthquake. From the morning of 12 August, for the next five days, 113 tremors reduced most of Cephallonia's 350 towns and villages to dust. About 85 per cent of Argostoli's buildings were destroyed. Around the island 600 people died; whole villages were abandoned, their residents never to

Right:
At Lassi, there is a simple memorial to the Italians slaughtered by the Germans in the Second World War

return. The first quake, registering 7.5 on the Richter Scale, with an estimated power of sixty-three atom bombs, equal to 1,750 million kWh, affected all of the island except the northern part, where Fiskardo remained largely untouched. The only positive outcome was that some of the islanders, having been warned the night before by a few tremors which destroyed neighbouring Itháki, had stayed outdoors.

The Greek newspaper *Ta Nea* recorded on its front page: 'A terrible earthquake which occurred at 11.27 today and lasted for 50 seconds completely destroyed the town of Argostoli.' As the news became known throughout the world help poured in from abroad. The British Navy were the first on the scene, clearing the rubble, building a tent city and providing food and water. Between August 1953 and April 1954, a further 3,000 tremors were recorded. Nowadays, all buildings have to be built to withstand earthquakes of over 8 on the Richter Scale.

Beta Galiatsatou describes the aftermath of the earthquake in her book *The Ghost Town*:

They were people but somehow they looked like something else. The dust had formed entire masks over their faces, and all that showed were two big eyes, horrified, and lips so pale and dry that you would think that life had left them long ago. Their bodies covered by half-torn clothes, they looked like dead bodies that had just been thrown from their graves, and without knowing what they wanted in this place they had found themselves in, they looked curiously at the demolished houses. Perhaps Dante would not have called on Virgil to be his imaginary companion in writing his famous Inferno, if he had lived for a short time during these moments in Argostoli. Moments of unbalance and madness ...

Opposite:
**Lighting candles
inside the church at
Omala during the
20 October
celebrations**

Around Argostoli

Situated on the Bay of Livadi, Argostoli has been the capital of the island since 1757. The area had always been used by fishermen and pirates, such as Barbarossa, when they used the island as a base for their marauding forays around the Mediterranean. In the fourteenth century, when raisins began to be exported, ships would also dock at a landing known as 'Peskaria' which later became today's harbour section.

Although the town has since lost many fine Venetian and nineteenth-century neo-classical buildings and churches, it still retains some of its old grandeur, and much of the shabby gentility of a typical working Greek town, particularly in some wide streets and squares, lined with palm trees and oleander bushes. This impression is also reinforced by its long water-front; apart from the noisy motorbikes and scooters that now puncture the air of Ioannis Metaxa Street that runs the length of the harbour, the scene has changed little since Napier described it so vividly in the 1820s:

The sounds of music, and of oars, with the song of boatmen, float along its smooth surface in the softness of a summer's evening with the most pleasing effect. The bright colours in which most southern nations love to dress, increase the liveliness of the scene; and added to the wildness of the overhanging mountains, with their changing evening tints, create a picture in which masses of rocks, water, and people are so grouped as to produce a beauty of scenery that this harbour has no claims to at any other period of the day, for the mountains which enclose the bay require the veil of their mists to soften their stern features.

Immediately after the 1953 earthquake, hastily constructed and inevitably ugly cement blocks were built everywhere, and these can

Opposite:
View of Argostoli,
the island's capital

Left:
Fishermen sell their daily catch at Argostoli's harbour quay

Right:

Farmers also bring in their produce to sell at the Saturday market in Argostoli

still be seen. There are also somewhat grander public buildings that were erected using some of the funds sent in the aftermath of the disaster by Cephallonians living abroad. These ex-patriots were keen to restore some of the island's dignity.

Much of Argostoli's action centres around the main Valianou Square, still one of the traditional meeting places for most inhabitants of the town on the traditional evening 'volta' (promenade),

together with the nearby well-kept gardens of Napier Park. The square is filled with outdoor cafés where people sit and consume *frappé* (iced coffees) and cakes, *periptera* (kiosks) selling newspapers and cigarettes, and some popular tavernas, open all the year round, that serve island specialities such as *kefallonitiki kreatopitta* (Cephallonian meat pie), *bourdetto* (fish stew) and *sofrito* (braised veal and garlic).

The waterfront and fish market

Like any island town, its nerve centre is around the waterfront market stalls and shops where farmers and fishermen bring their produce to sell every morning. They are close to where the old Venetian warehouses once stood, filled with the island's 'black gold', the raisins that became renowned throughout Europe. Today, they are still available, along with bottles of the island's famous wine, Robola. Here, there is also a string of decent *kafeneia* (cafés) and ouzeries, widely used by the market and fisher folk, serving fiery carafes of *ouzo* and *mezedes*.

As in most of the Greek islands, fishing plays an important role in Cephallonia. The island's long and craggy coastline, scattered with small inlets and coves, is ideal for the caiques and small boats that set their nets on a daily basis unless the weather forces them to stay in port. Much of what is caught makes its way to the main fish market which is situated next to the waterfront. The early-morning catches are eagerly awaited by the fishmongers, taverna owners, and housewives who wander down almost immediately after the larger caiques arrive back in port. Rusty scales are brought out by the fishermen who sell their catches from the quayside; others send wooden boxes of fish, packed with crushed ice, straight to the market to be auctioned to the highest bidder. Some of the more expensive fish, such as *xiphias* (swordfish), *barbounia* (red mullet), *tonnos* (tuna) and *synagrida* (dentex) make their way to the mainland's fish markets in Patras, Piraeus and Athens. There is plenty of demand for the rest, especially in the summer when visitors clamour for fresh fish at beach tavernas all around the island.

Behind the waterfront municipal market is the Lithostroto. Still the

Left:
Only the first storey remains of this elegant Argostoli mansion after the 1953 earthquake

main shopping street, filled with clothes, jewellery and tourist stores, it also contains three important churches: the church of Aghios Spiridon (Corfu's patron saint) which has an annual procession on 12 August to commemorate the 1953 earthquake; the Roman Catholic church of Aghios Nikolaos with an impressive bell tower; and the Greek Orthodox Metropolis (cathedral) of Aghios Georgios, built in 1957.

Museums and theatre

Nearby are the island's main museums. Despite its unfavourable exterior, the Archaeological Museum on Rokou Vergoti Street contains some interesting exhibits: finds from the Sanctuary of Pan in Mellisani Lake; a third-century BC tomb from Kombothekrata containing a male and a female skeleton; Mycenaean jewellery and vases; bronze swords and coins from the four ancient city states of the island.

Above the museum the historic Kefalos Theatre has been rebuilt after being destroyed by German incendiary bombs in the Second World War. The island's first theatre, it was founded by public subscription in 1857. Its opening production, in 1859, was Verdi's *La Traviata*, performed by Venice's La Fenice Opera. Until the early twentieth century, local audiences were treated to many works – often subversive – by local playwrights.

Close by in Ilia Zervou Street is the Corgialenios Historical and Cultural Museum. The ground-floor Corgialenios Library and Concert Hall, with a collection of nearly 50,000 manuscripts and books, was built in 1924 from a legacy bequeathed by Marinos Corgialenios, and is one of the few elegant mansions to survive the earthquake. The basement Corgialenios Museum, located beneath the Library, was established in the 1960s by

ARGOSTOLI. Belfry and entrance to St. Gerasimo's abbey.

Left:
An old postcard of
Aghios Gerasimos
monastery at Omala

the resourceful Helen Cosmetatos, and offers an enterprising collection of local ephemera, religious icons and screens, and family heirlooms from leading families. These reveal the island's rich social and cultural traditions that developed in the nineteenth century. The household items and finery brought back from European ports bear witness to the island's strong seafaring traditions: there is delicate lace from Flanders; Parisian ball-gowns; fine porcelain and china from Italy and France. Of particular interest are the archive photographs of the island as it was in 1904 and some harrowing documentation of the effects of the 1953 earthquake.

Right:

Making beeswax candles for the Greek Easter celebrations

The ancient site of Krane

Beyond the Koutavos Lagoon, at Razata, is the site of Krane, or Krani. Huge, lichened rocks litter the hillside, all that remains of the ancient city state. Further up the hillside there are some fifth-century BC tombs, the 'Drakospilia' ('dragon's cave'), a rectangular tomb carved out of the rock that probably dates from the Roman period, and fragments of a Doric temple dedicated to Demeter. But it is the massive slabs of remaining polygonal seventh-century BC Cyclopean walls that attract attention. A few are just as D.T. Ansted saw them in 1863:

In Cranea, the most perfect remains are those that run down the side of one hill, and up another, on the east side; and of these, the walls at the southern end are the most modern, and in best condition. All this wall is very remarkable for the number of projections or towers with which it is defended. The foundations of many of these are in good condition, and they seem to show that the line of fortification consisted of a number of towers, about eight yards square, connected by a strong wall, and was not merely a continuous wall. It is also clear that this part of the wall was extremely thick. The polygonal work in Cranea is, perhaps, more perfect and gigantic than in any part of the Ionian islands.

The Lassi peninsula

From the harbour, the coastal road also snakes around a wooded headland to the pleasant Lassi peninsula, Aghios Theodori lighthouse and the famous Katouvres ('swallow holes'). This curious phenomenon, whereby strong currents of sea water ran through 100-foot rock channels, was utilized by the English in the nineteenth century to power water mills. Before the Second World War, an ice-making factory and electricity power plant also ran off the water system until the 1953 earthquake dried up the channels. One of the mills has been rebuilt, although its wooden paddles are more for show, as they rarely work with the small amount of water available today.

For a long time scientists tried to discover just where the water disappeared to on the island. It wasn't until 1963 that an Austrian team of scientists solved the mystery by pouring strong dyes into the channels. The water, combining with rainwater seeping through the island's mountain chains, resurfaced on the other side of the island near Sami in the Mellisani caves, and off the coast at Karavomylos.

Left:
A girl with spring lambs

Opposite:
A church on Good Friday during Greek Easter

Around the Island

South-east of Argostoli the road towards the Livatho region passes through the Lassi peninsula. There are two excellent beaches here, Makris Gialos and Platis Gialos. Ending in the rocky promontory of Tourkopodaro, they have helped to make the region the island's most built-up tourist area, filled with large hotels, bouzouki bars and plate-smashing nightclubs. The cave of Aghios Gerasimos is also located here at Spilia. In 1555, Gerasimos, the island's patron saint, arrived from Zakynthos, and spent five years living in the cave as a hermit before founding the Monastery at Omala that now bears his name. Today, converted into a small whitewashed chapel, its interior blackened by candle smoke, it has become a popular place of pilgrimage.

The Livatho region

This has always been the island's most highly populated and prosperous area. It is filled with some charming villages where the local Cephallonian aristocracy, mostly merchants and sea captains, built their fine mansions. Here they farmed the surrounding fertile fields and the hills covered with vineyards, citrus and olive groves. There are some ancient, beautifully gnarled olive trees in the area, testimony to centuries of cultivation. Local legend has it that in 1537 a Cephallonian woman called Diatsenta threw herself off one of the limestone cliffs close to the village of Minies to escape the clutches of the pirate Barbarossa. Despite the airport's neces-sary and noisy location here, the villages and fields are all still thriving.

Nearby vineyards belong to Nicholas Cosmetatos, who in 1978 built a winery and house perched on the cliffs. From the grapes two of Greece's enterprising new white wines are produced: Gentilini (made from 100 per cent Robola grapes) and Gentilini Fumé (a blend of 60 per cent

Opposite:
Petani bay on the north-west coast of the Paliki peninsula

Sauvignon Blanc and 40 per cent Chardonnay aged in casks) have won many international awards. Minies is also the site of a small sixth-century BC Doric temple and the seventeenth-century church of Theotokos Mangana. During the Second World War, the curator of Argostoli's Corgialenios Museum, Helen Cosmetatos, together with her husband, successfully hid John Capes, the only survivor of the mined submarine *HMS Perseus*, in their house in the village. He managed to escape detection by hiding under the floorboards.

South of Minies, the road passes through the attractive villages of Sarlata, Svoronata, Domata and Kalligata. Sarlata has an old bell tower that still stands, despite the earthquake, and Domata is home to the church of Theotokos or Panagia (the Virgin Mary). Inside there is an impressive gilded wooden iconostasis (altar screen) that dates from the nineteenth century: 12,000 gold sovereigns were melted down to use for the gilt. There are also some notable Russian icons and the remains of the martyr patriarch Gregory V. Hanged by the Turks on 10 April 1821,

his body was found floating in the Bosphorus by a Cephallonian sea captain, Nikolaos Sklavos, who took the remains to Odessa for burial before transporting the coffin back to the island. Gregory's feast day is celebrated every year on 10 April. It is worth taking a walk around some of Domata's side streets where there are some good examples of abandoned pre-earth-

Opposite:

Goats on one of the dirt-track roads on Mount Aenos

Right:

A mountain goat on the roadside near Myrtos beach

quake neo-classical mansions. The village also contains, reputedly, the island's oldest olive tree, known locally as the 'chatting tree', which seats twenty people inside its hollow trunk.

The precipitous cliffs of the nearby Cape Aghia Pelagia and Cape Liakas, and beaches such as Ai-Heli, Avithos and Spartia, are probable settings for some of the scenes in *Captain Corelli's Mandolin* when Pelagia gazes wistfully at Mandras as he swims with the dolphins or prepares for fishing trips. The sheer coastline is dramatic, and the caves below are said to have hidden British submarines during the Second World War. During the war, the British dropped cans of gold sovereigns, intended for resistance fighters, in the fields around the area. Some local farmers have benefited considerably from their unexpected harvest when tilling the fields.

Giant aloe plants, swaying bamboo and banana trees, yellow and purple flowers of broom and Judas trees all contribute to the beauty. Opposite is the tiny islet of Dias, reached by boat, especially on 2 July every year, when the locals celebrate the feast day of the Panagia Vlachernon chapel which was rebuilt after the 1953 earthquake by the Vallianos ship-owning family from the village of Keramies. Celebrations take place at Avithos beach and on the island. Spartia has an illustrious merchant navy tradition. In the nineteenth century, it had a fleet of ninety ships that plied the Mediterranean and Black Seas from the coves beneath the village. It is also the birthplace of Vangelis Panas, one of the leaders of Cephallonian forces during the 1821 War of Independence.

Kalligata is home to the eighteenth-century church of Theotokos, with its fine belfry and carved gilded iconostasis, and to the Calligas winery. Founded in the early 1960s by two cousins, Gerasimos and Yiannis Calligas, the company makes some interesting red and white table wines,

Opposite:
The Melissani cave is reached by a short boat ride

such as the familiar Robola, Château Calligas and Rubis. Their vineyards are located at Razata and Frangata in the Omala valley where there is an annual wine festival held on the first Saturday after 15 August.

There are three other villages of note: Lakithra, Kourkoumelata, and Metaxata. Lakithra, the old capital of the Livatho area, was rebuilt with French donations after the earthquake. Near its church of Aghios Nikolaos ton Aliprantidon, Professor Spyridon Marinatos discovered, in the 1930s, four late-Mycenaean tombs and antique grain silos hewn out of the rock. Another archaeologist, Professor A. Goekoop, claims this to be the site of Odysseus's palace.

Kourkoumelata was rebuilt courtesy of a local benefactor, George Vergotis, who styled many of the houses on a typical Swiss town, except for the rather out-of-place, and immaculate, neo-classical building of the Cultural Centre.

Metaxata is famous mostly for being a temporary home for Lord Byron. In 1823, he rented a house for four months, unfortunately destroyed by the earthquake, before departing for his ill-fated trip to Missolonghi where he died soon afterwards. At Lakithra, on a rock in an area where he used to enjoy sitting, look for the marble plaque commemorating his short but influential stay on the island with the words from a poem he wrote: 'If I am a poet, I owe it to the air of Greece.'

The Monastery of Aghiou Apostolou Andrea and the Castle of St George

Inland from these villages lie the important Monastery of Aghiou Apostolou Andrea Milapidias at Peratata, and the historic Castle of St George. Founded in the Byzantine era in the sixth or seventh century, the

monastery is first referred to as the Monastery of Apostolou Andrea in 1264. For several hundred years it lay deserted until 1579, when three nuns, Benedict, Leondia and Magdalena, bought the land surrounding the ruined chapel and established a nunnery. In 1639, Princess Roxanne, daughter of an Epirote nobleman, began her monastic life here as the renamed nun Romila. She donated much of her wealth to the nunnery, including a relic from Mount Athos – a dried fragment of the crucified St Andrew's right foot. There is an ecclesiastical museum in the old Katholikon, the only building that survived the earthquake. It contains restored thirteenth-century frescoes, icons, relics, and an intricate hand-painted iconostasis. There are two annual feast days: 30 November for St Andrew, and the Friday after Easter for the feast day of Zoodochous Pigi, with processions following the nunnery's various holy relics into the chapel of St Nicholas.

Opposite are the ruins of the Castle of St George, San Giorgio as the Venetians called it, or Kastro as it is known today, 320 metres above sea level. With its commanding view, it was an obvious choice as Cephallonia's citadel capital, and from 1500 until 1759 it was home to all the island's rulers and nobility and it once had a population of 14,000 living within the safety of its strong walls. After the two-month siege of 1500, when the Turks were successfully ousted, it was rebuilt in 1504 by Venetian and Greek craftsmen, under the direction of Nikolaos Tsimaras.

Little remains of its outbuildings, such as hospital, barracks and store-

Left:
At the church of Zoodochous Pigi in Arginia, a priest eats a bowl of mutton soup prepared at a festival on the Friday after Easter

Right:
The festival procession of the icon outside the small church of Zoodochous Pigi in Arginia

houses, although its imposing gateway and ramp, Venetian coats-of-arms, polygonal fortifications, not to mention its size – 1,600 square metres – can still be seen. Inside, in the castle's small square, are the remains of a Catholic church. A little further down the hill, the church of the Evangelistria, built in 1580, was the island's old cathedral. Its rather grand Corinthian arched doorway is still standing. Also nearby are the Mazarakata rock tombs. This Mycenaean necropolis of eighty-three graves, including a characteristic 'Tholos' beehive tomb, was excavated in 1908 by the archaeologist P. Kavadias. It yielded much pottery, gold jewellery and other grave offerings on display in Argostoli's Archaeological Museum.

From here the coastal road to Skala, on the south-eastern tip of the island, passes through Lourdata. Its long, thin strip of beach was much favoured by the British in the nineteenth century, and it is said to derive its name after the Lords who enjoyed its mild summer climate. There is a huge, ancient plane tree in the village square and a spring whose stone troughs were once used by the village women on washdays.

Sheltered by Mount Aenos, Lourdata enjoys a microclimate that enables many tropical plants to grow. You can take an invigorating walk through the maquis, on the island's first nature trail, created with funds from the World Wildlife Fund. It leads to the thirteenth-century Monastery of Sission, close to Vlachata where old terraced fields tumble to the sea. Said to have been founded by St Francis of Assisi, its name is an obvious corruption of Assisi. In 1218, returning from the Crusades in Egypt, a bad storm forced Francis' ship to stop, and he founded a monastery at this spot. Abandoned in the sixteenth century, it then became an orthodox monastery. Sadly it was destroyed by the 1953 earthquake, but its ruins

are visible today beneath the new monastery building. Some of its important icons by the seventeenth-century Cretan artist-monk Stefanos Tzankarolas are on display in Peratata's monastery of Aghiou Apostolou Andrea. There is an annual procession from the church of Evangelistria to the monastery of Sission with one of its old icons.

At Markopoulo, one of the island's most famous religious events occurs at the church of the Panagia Langouvarda. Every year at the beginning of August, harmless snakes with crosses on their heads 'miraculously' appear in time for the festival of Dormition of the Virgin which takes place on 15 August. The snakes enter the church and curl themselves around the silver icon of the Panagia Fidou ('Virgin of the snakes'). Then they disappear again until the next year. Sceptics claim that the church is merely on their annual migratory path. Nowadays, the villagers collect the snakes beforehand to make sure that they appear for the crowds. Dr Loukatos, in his book Summertime Customs, writes:

What can one say about these snakes ? If one believes in miracles, there is nothing to be said. But if one tries to find a natural explanation, one might assume that they are a non-poisonous variety of snake which thrived and multiplied in that region, first because the climate suited them, and second because the villagers never harmed them. Through heredity they became accustomed to man, as man did to them, so they do not fear each other. It is possible that around the 15 August festivities, their mating and egg-laying season occurs. That fact, together with the sounds of ringing bells and the noises of the crowd may make them come out of their nests. Unprotestingly and trustingly, they allow themselves to be handled by humans.

Left:

In the hills above Sami, the ancient ruins of the Cyatis acropolis were incorporated into a Byzantine church

Skala has been popular since the Roman period. It is the site of a third-century AD villa, with well-preserved mosaics that were excavated in 1957, and its beaches, Kato Katelios and Potomakia, keep it even busier today. A few kilometres south of Ratzakli, Potomakia is, along with some beaches on neighbouring Zakynthos, one of the main annual nesting grounds for loggerhead turtles (*Caretta caretta*). Another endangered species, the Mediterranean monk seal (*Monachus monachus*), is also present on the island. Seals inhabit some of the sea caves on the east coast of the island. Fewer than 500 of these seals exist worldwide, making it one of the world's rarest mammals, and there is an estimated population of 250 in Greece. Although they are unpopular with local fishermen because of their prodigious appetites, efforts to preserve them by the Hellenic Society for the Study and Protection of the Monk Seal (HSSPMS) seem to be paying off.

Destroyed completely by the 1953 earthquake, Skala is unremarkable today except for its position at the tip of the island, and for some spectacular views towards the Gulf of Patras. Just two miles north of Skala, under the chapel of Aghios Georgios, there are the foundations of a seventh-century BC temple to Apollo, another reputed spot where the crusaders used to stop for water on their long sea voyages. Parts of the temple were used to build the small chapel above. Behind Skala, in the hills above the village of Pastra, there are also the scant remains of some of the polygonal walls of the ancient city of Pronoi, known locally

as 'Kastro tis Sirias' ('castle of the beautiful maiden'). Pastra is also the site of the church of Panagia Gravaliotissa where Madonna lilies miraculously bloom every year on 15 August.

Further north, past Asprogerakas – another village that was abandoned after the 1953 earthquake – lies Tzanata, where some substantial Mycenaean tombs and artefacts were found during excavations by Greek and Danish archaeologists in June 1991. In particular, the large domed 'Tholos' beehive tomb discovered by the Patras archaeologist Professor Kolonas, caused yet more speculation that this could be the site of Odysseus' tomb and citadel. Inland from Tzanata, there is a stunning, if somewhat bumpy, drive along an untarmacked road through the foothills of Mount Aenos, to the mountain villages of Kapandriti and Xenopoulo, where ancient threshing floors and fields, tumbling dry-stone walls and paint-blistered farm gates litter the small plain.

Poros, as one of the closest gateways to the mainland, has always been an important port. It is reached through a narrow gorge between steep cliffs, called the 'Arakli gap'. According to popular legend, the gorge was carved by the footprints of the impetuous Hercules. With its long sweep of shingle beach, Poros has also recently developed as one of the island's chief resorts.

Above the thriving town, a steep and winding drive up Mount Atrous takes the visitor to the island's oldest monastery. The Monastery of Theotokos Atrou is located 760 metres above sea level. Built in the Byzantine era, around the eighth century AD, it is first mentioned in records of 1248. Although badly damaged by the earthquake, a tower dating from the Middle Ages still stands.

Right:

Checking inside
the bee hives

Left:
Interior of a small
roadside shrine in
Assos containing
wicks and olive oil
for its primitive oil
lamp

The Rakli valley

Northwards towards Sami, in the Pirgi region, is the fertile Rakli valley where villages, such as Aghios Nikolaos, are irrigated by Lake Avitho which takes its name from the ancient belief that it was 'bottomless'. D.T. Ansted travelled here in 1863:

'The vale of Rakli is one of the richest and most important valleys, being connected with Samos on the north, and with the sea, with little interruption on the south. It contains some natural curiosities, and amongst them are deep pools always filled with water. Some of these pools are of considerable size, and the following description of one of them, from Dr Davy's account of the Ionian islands, will be read with pleasure: 'In a wild valley, contiguous to that of Samos, at a higher level, is a small lake, known by the name of Abatho, signifying bottomless, which it is supposed to be by the natives. It is circular, about two hundred yards in circumference, and is surrounded by rugged hills, composed chiefly of clay, conglomerate, and sandstone. A small stream constantly flows from it, most copious in winter, which joins another small stream, flowing from a similar little lake, separated by an intervening hill, and these two streams joining from the river of Rakli, the principal perennial stream of Cephalonia.'

Sami is the island's second largest port, well laid out after the earthquake with spacious squares, gardens and a long quay with decent tavernas and cafés. Behind the modern town, in the foothills of Aghii Fanentes and Kastro, are the remains of Same, one of the most important of the four ancient city states. Overgrown somewhat by vegetation today, the remains still give some sense of the sheer size of the citadel, with its

twenty-two entrances and massive walls, interspersed with buildings and towers from the Roman period. Of chief interest are some of the massive stones used for the walls, some of them two cubic yards in size, perfectly squared and bevelled, each weighing about three tons. As D.T. Ansted notes:

When we find that not one is chipped or injured, that they lie one on the other so closely, that though there is no mortar it would be impossible to pass a long thin blade of grass between them, and that during the two thousand years that have elapsed since the town was attacked and taken by the Romans, vegetation has failed to penetrate the narrow crevices in those parts that are still perfect – when we further see that water has failed to injure them, and that they remain as they always were, we almost doubt whether they will ever change.

Lower down are the remains of some Roman baths, known as 'Rakospiti' (a corruption of 'Drakospiti' or 'dragon's cave'), where the mosaic fragment of Poseidon and a superb bronze Roman head were discovered in the 1950s. Both can now be seen in Argostoli's Archaeological Museum.

Agrillion monastery is also hidden in the hills above Sami. It was built

Left:
**An old set of scales
inside the Café
Caruso in Komitata**

Opposite:
**A villager in Skala
lighting a fire in the
old oven**

Opposite:
**A shepherd's tools
outside his hut near
Arginia**

Right:
**A farmer with his
collection of hand-
carved walking
sticks in Melissani**

in the eighteenth century, on the spot where, in 1722, two shepherds found an icon in the olive groves, close to the deserted Byzantine monastery of Aghios Phanedon that was built on the old city walls of Same. Destroyed by the earthquake, the monastery church has now been rebuilt in honour of St Cosmas the Aetolian, who preached his ascetic sermons on the island in 1777. A procession on his feast day is held every year on 24 August. In 1823, Byron stayed at the monastery. In some of the remaining monastery buildings, there is a narrow white-washed room, with rafters across its low ceiling, that is supposed to be his guest chamber, graced by his portrait. The monastery tower still stands but is not safe to climb; its three bells hang below the branches of a gnarled olive tree just as they did when Byron first visited this picturesque place. Beneath the monastery, Anti Samos is a beautiful sandy beach, rimmed by trees, and reached by a dirt-track road.

Sami is also close to the island's impressive caves, a complex system of limestone caves, underground lakes and streams where much of the water from Argostoli's sinkholes ('katouvres') reappears. Most have steep cave entrances, such as Angalaki, Hiridoni, Aghii Theodori, Zervati and Aghia Elousa, leading to underwater caverns and lakes that are off-limits to the general public. Close to the village of Karavomylos, with its circular lake, the Melissani cave is one of the island's most famous tourist attractions. After the 1953 earthquake, its roof caved in, allowing the sun's rays to filter through and reflect a myriad array of shimmering purple, indigo and blue colours all around. Reached by a short boat ride, the main cave chamber is over 160 metres in length. Excavations in 1951 and 1963 also unearthed evidence that it was an early sanctuary to the god Pan. A clay figurine of the god, a fragment of a nymph in bas-

relief and an unusual disc of Pan surrounded by nymphs, are all on display in the Archaeological Museum.

Just north of here, Aghia Evfimia is a charming port. Facing the island of Ithaki, it was rebuilt, after the earthquake, to its original 1878 town plans, with the help of French funds. Above the port, the picturesque village of Drakopoulata was one of the few in Cephallonia to escape the earthquake's devastation. Inland, off the main road to Argostoli at Chaliotata, Drogerati is another notable cave, discovered in the last century. About 123 steps lead down to its illuminated chamber which is over 100 metres square. Concerts are often given here and Maria Callas once performed amidst the colourful stalactites and stalagmites of the chamber, with its eerily excellent acoustics.

Mount Aenos

There are two approaches, on the main road from Sami to Argostoli, to Mount Aenos, the island's celebrated mountain whose summit area was declared a National Park in 1962. The first, winding through the maquis, reaches the Agrapidies Pass (550 metres) before ending up at a radar station. The summit of Megas Soros (1,628 metres), the highest point of the imposing mountain range, can also be reached from here. From the top of Megas Soros, Henry Napier, who visited his brother Colonel Charles Napier in the 1820s, recorded: 'The highest point of this mountain is 5,380 feet above the sea. It springs up boldly with an abruptness that would prove inaccessible to anything but a goat. This is curious because a hill of such altitude seldom rises on so small a base. Fourteen miles in length, its width is perhaps not more than three.' Beneath its summit, there are also the remains of a sanctuary dedicated to Zeus.

Left:
Freshly prepared goats' cheeses in a shepherd's hut near Arginia

Right:
**An old-style village
kitchen with a
bamboo shelf to
mature cheeses
hanging from the
ceiling**

The second approach is through the fertile Omalos valley and the Monastery of Aghios Gerasimos, where vineyards and olive groves surround the villages of Frangata and Valsamata, rebuilt with British funds after the earthquake. From here, another road leads southwards to the Castle of St George, via the villages of Troianata and Demoutsanata. At Demoutsanata's church of Agii Paraskevi, there is another of the island's strange religious events. Every year, on 23 August, another lily miraculously blooms in front of an icon to the Virgin.

Pilgrims come from all over Greece to visit the monastery of Aghios Gerasimos. At the end of an expansive tree-lined drive, a modern church built in 1992 and bell tower greet visitors, although the old monastic enclosures have been converted into pleasant gardens and vegetable plots by the nuns who live there. Aghios Gerasimos is so popular that he has two annual feast days, celebrated throughout the island with often Bacchanalian excess and bravado. One is on 16 August, the day after he died, and the other on 20 October, when his relics were originally removed from his tomb.

A small church, the monastery's oldest surviving building, has been built over the cave where Aghios Gerasimos lived. His remains, encased in an ornate silver reliquary, are kept near the iconostasis, close to an iron ladder that descends into the cave. On the feast days, the sarcophagus is taken, by a procession, to one of the three massive plane trees that he

Opposite:
A man cleans
freshly picked
'horta' (wild greens)
from the fields

planted amidst the forty wells that he dug with his own hands in this previously arid spot. Born in Trikala in 1507 to wealthy refugees from Constantinople, the island's patron saint Gerasimos Notaras was ordained in Mount Athos, travelled to Crete and Zakynthos, and studied in Jerusalem for twelve years before arriving on the island in 1555. After his first five years in the cave at Spilia, he founded a nunnery at Omala in 1560, naming it 'New Jerusalem', and spent his time teaching the children of the local villages. After he died in 1579, so-called miracles began to occur, and when his remains were exhumed a few years later, on 20 October 1581, they had not decomposed. He was canonized in 1622. Since then he has been known especially for reputedly being able to cure mental illness and exorcize demons.

Snow-covered for much of the year, Mount Aenos was the island's most famous source of wealth. Its legendary forest of pine trees, the indigenous Cephallonian fir (*Abies Cephalonica*) once blanketed the entire mountain. The mountain was also home to mythological dragons and demons; wild horses, of which a few still survive; rare flora, such as a species of autumn-flowering snowflake (*Leucojum valentinium*); and mountain herbs which were collected to make potions and treatments, macerated or infused with wine or spirits to make potent local liqueurs such as *Rosalia*. The mountain was also renowned for its ice, collected by men and women and removed to natural caves and artificial ice houses for use all year round. Cephallonia supplied all the neighbouring islands, especially Zante, with ice.

From a distance, the bushy, silvery firs, with upward-pointing branches, once gave the island the appearance of being covered in a dark cloak, hence its ancient name of *Melaina* ('black') and Venetian name of

Monte Nero ('Black Mountain'). Both were also other names for Cephallonia. *Abies Cephalonica*, known as *pitys* to the ancients, is also found in some other parts of Greece at heights over 800 metres, although it is mostly associated with Cephallonia. Sir Charles Napier also managed to establish the growth of the tree from seedlings in England. The fir was consecrated by the ancients to Pan, god of shepherds. According to ancient mythology, both Pan and Boreas, the north wind, were trying to woo the nymph Pitys. She preferred Pan to Boreas who then blew her off a cliff. When Pan located her lifeless body, he promptly changed her into a fir tree. The resin that seeps out of the cones whenever the north wind blows is supposed to be the nymph's tears.

The fast-growing tree produces strong and straight timber, and was crucial to boat-building, both for the maritime ancient Greeks' triremes, and the Venetians' galleons. The Venetians also used the wood to build fortresses. Homer mentions that the oars of Odysseus' boats were made from the pine. Columns from Crete's Palace of Knossos have been identified as coming from the tree, and even Napoleon, when he met the Cephallonian Marino Metaxas, immediately enquired about the forest, such was its fame and importance to empire-builders. By the sixteenth century, the forest itself was about fourteen kilometres in length and five kilometres in width. Despite later attempts by the Venetians to protect the forest, they are responsible for most of the rapacious over-felling of trees. By 1501, they had settled over 200 wood-cutters and carpenters in the forest. Forest fires, both natural and deliberately started, also diminished its size dramatically. The worst occurred in 1590, 1730, 1760, 1793 and 1797, changing the island's climate and destroying over nine-tenths of the forest. The fire of 1793 was started accidentally by peasants who

Opposite:
Detail of a well-used donkey saddle

Opposite:
**Fishermen take
freshly caught
whitebait from the
net in Argostoli
harbour**

had illegally rented the land from the Venetian consul Bortolo Cingani, and who were trying to clear it to plant wheat. It raged for months and darkened the skies over Argostoli.

By the time the British arrived the damage had been done. Attempts at conservation were always hampered by the indiscriminate grazing by goats of seedlings and small trees. As Napier observed:

In Cephalonia, it is quite impossible to preserve trees, as the goats destroy them all and are rapidly annihilating the public forests on the Black Mountain which forests would be a source of great wealth to the island if protected; but thousands of goats prevent the growth of every thing like a plantation and what is worse, are the cause of more litigation, ill blood, crime and idleness, than any other source of mischief in the island, neither vineyards, fields, nor gardens can escape the devastations of these animals, as it is impossible to make any sufficient fence to exclude them.

Napier's attempts were also largely frustrated by Sir Frederick Adam's indifference to the problem. He notes in his diary:

The forest is of vital importance. Yet Sir Frederick prefers to listen to the goat herds rather than his representatives. The goat herds are rich and powerful and there is no doubt convinced His Excellency that the forest was useless and that animal husbandry was profitable. One of these told me in all sincerity that if the tips of young pines were nibbled by the goats they would grow faster and develop into flourishing trees. I presume that their viewpoint has been accepted because the forest has since been abandoned. That the forest has been neglected is proof that the shepherd's view was accepted as opposed to that of his staff.

The mountain is also a bird-watcher's paradise with many migratory birds finding temporary refuge in its forest. Amongst the black-eared wheateaters (*Oenanthe hispanica*), blue rock thrushes (*Monticola solitarius*), Bonelli's warblers (*Phylloscopus bonelli*), mistle thrushes (*Turdus viscivorus*), goldcrests (*Regulus regulus*), jays (*Garrulus glandarius*) and robins (*Erithacus rubecula*) that all nest, there are rare black woodpeckers (*Dryocopus martius*) and white-backed woodpeckers (*Dendrocopos leucotos*), huge eagle owls (*Bubo bubo*) and Tengmalm's owls (*Aegolius funereus*). Magnificent birds of prey, such as griffon vultures (*Gyps fulvus*), golden eagles (*Aquila chrysaetos*), goshawks (*Accipiter gentilis*), short-toed eagles (*Circaetus gallicus*), long-legged buzzards (*Buteo rufinus*) and Eleonora's falcons (*Falco eleonorae*) also inhabit the heights.

From Argostoli to Fiskardo, the twisting road to the island's north-west Erissos peninsula is an often stunning clifftop drive. Stop at Farsa and wander the quiet streets and houses of the old village on the hill. Deserted since the 1953 earthquake, this is where Louis de Bernières, wandering around these sad ruins, first conceived *Captain Corelli's Mandolin*. Some excellent pristine beaches are along this stretch. At Kardakata, the turn-off for Lixouri and the Paliki peninsula, the road passes through the village of Zola, before snaking down to the beach of Aghia Kyriaki where a taverna, small fishing harbour and long shingle beach await. Another road goes back up to Angonas, where there are some lurid, naive wall paintings by a local artist, 'Razos', on whitewashed walls in the village square.

At Siniori, there is also a road inland towards the villages of the Pilarou

Right:
Kyria Labroula from
the village of Farsa.
She hid two Italians
down her well
during the War

Left:
Detail of the
window of a house
in Assos

Right:
A blackboard menu
of a village
kafeneion

region and Aghia Evfimia on the east coast. In the hills around the Pilarou villages, many of the goats look as though they have silver- or gold-plated teeth because of the mica content of the soil and plants. North of Aghia Evfimia is another old monastery. Near the village of Makryotica, the Monastery of Theotokos Thematon, located amidst a forest of Kermes oak trees, was founded in the twelfth century. It was rebuilt in 1970, and there is an annual festival on the first Sunday after Easter. Just after Divarata, there is one of the best beaches in Greece, reached by a four-kilometre descent of tight hairpin turns. Viewed from the road above, the turquoise waters that fringe Myrtos beach's long swathe of sand and pebbles are always irresistible.

Just over the headland at Myrtos is the port of Assos. Built beneath a rocky peninsula, Assos' two harbours straddle an isthmus. One of the prettiest modern villages in Cephallonia, it was rebuilt with French aid after the earthquake. Its red-roofed houses, narrow whitewashed streets and sleepy cafés are often quiet, as there are few rooms to rent here and it has mercifully avoided the package-tourist hordes. At the small village square by the harbour, named Platia Parison ('Paris Square') in gratitude to the French, there is an ancient olive tree where St Cosmas used to preach. From here, it is a short walk to the Assos fortress. Built by the Venetians in 1593, it remained the seat of the local Venetian *providore* until 1797. Napier was so enamoured with the fortress that he likened it to 'a second Gibraltar and even stronger than Gibraltar'. Inside there were once sixty public buildings and 200 private homes protected from the frequent pirate raids. Entering the arched main gate, the visitor sees the remains of the church of San Marco built in 1604, the Governor's house, the barracks and a prison that was in use until 1815. The local Destounis family also inhabited the fortress until 1968 and some of their graves can be seen in the church of Profitis Elias.

Fiskardo

At the northernmost tip of the island, the village of Fiskardo, surrounded by groves of cypress trees, is for many people the most picturesque village on the island, although tourism takes its toll in the summer months. Decreed a traditional village by the Greek Government in 1975, its character is now protected by stringent building restrictions. Unscathed by the earthquakes, it is a mecca for visitors, with its small nineteenth-century neo-classical sea captain's mansions, painted in faded pink and ochre colours, encircling a shallow harbour filled in the summer with a flotilla of yachts. It is a perfect port for reflective idling at one of the cafés while enjoying a carafe of ouzo; sitting on a balcony reading a book; watching the sunset sitting on a rock with feet dangling in the crystal-clear waters; or fishing with the locals for *kefalos* (grey mullet) by day and *soupies* (cuttlefish) by night as they come close to shore.

Known as Panormos in ancient times, the village is surrounded by important archaeological remains. Mycenaean objects have been found in the hills above nearby Emblissi beach; Roman tombs and baths dating from the second century AD, including four stone sarcophagi carved with images of Artemis, stand in an enclosure next to the town's Panormos Hotel, and there are the foundations of a Byzantine church on the site of Fiskardo's main church of Panagia tis Platiteras. Towards the Venetian lighthouse on the Fournias headland, there are more interesting archaeological remains. Said to be built on the earlier site of a temple to Apollo, the ruins of a sixth-century Byzantine church can be seen. At its entrance

Opposite:
Men playing cards in the old *kafeneion* beside the causeway in Argostoli

Left:
Detail of a boat
rudder painted with
a mermaid in Aghia
Evfimia

are also two Norman towers. Nearby there is a depression carved into the rock, believed to be a sacrificial altar, and known locally as the 'Throne of the Queen of Fiskarda'. Within sight of nearby Ithaki on the south-east coast, there are innumerable tree-lined coves. Here also is Daskalio, the small island between Cephallonia and Ithaki thought to be Homer's Asteris island where the courtiers awaited the return of Odysseus. Further along this coast, at Vari, there is the late-Byzantine cruciform church of Panagia Kougiana, with frescos of heaven and hell painted by a local artist. Unfortunately, since the villagers whitewashed one wall of the painting, only the frescos of hell remain.

Lixouri

All year round, ferries regularly cross from Argostoli to Lixouri, the island's second largest town, and capital of the wild Paliki peninsula. Often forgotten by visitors, this region has some lively working villages in its rugged hills, strange rock formations and beaches carved out of the gypsum and limestone on its south coast, and is the most intensely farmed area of the island. Vines, olives, citrus fruits and vegetable crops are all cultivated in its fertile fields.

Founded in 1534, Lixouri is still an attractive town, despite its destruction by earthquakes in 1867 and 1953. Sadly, Kennedy and Napier's 'Markato' building has been lost but the town's wide tree-lined streets and squares manage to create a sense of order and space. By the harbour, a statue of Andreas Laskaratos (1811–1901), resplendent in top hat and coat, greets visitors. Laskaratos was famed throughout Greece as a poet and intellectual who made savage and satirical attacks on the Orthodox Church. His is just one of many statues of illustrious citizens scattered

throughout the town. Many were politicians or benefactors who rebuilt its schools and hospitals, donated their libraries, and established the strong cultural traditions that still exist today. The town is home to the Palli Philharmonic, the second oldest orchestral school in Greece, and music clubs that specialize in the island's unique, unaccompanied arietta and cantata choral forms.

One of the few buildings to survive the earthquake is the Lakovatos Mansion, built in the 1860s. Now a library and museum, its fourteen rooms, all with intricate painted ceilings and furnishings, house a unique collection of over 30,000 rare books and manuscripts – including tenth- and fourteenth-century illuminated manuscripts and gospels – icons and ecclesiastical vestments, belonging to the distinguished Typaldos-Iakovatos family of doctors, lawyers, clerics and politicians who originally came from Naples in the fourteenth century.

Ever since the Venetians made Argostoli the island capital, the political and cultural rivalry between the two towns has been intense. During the French occupation in 1800, Lixouri briefly became an alternative capital to Argostoli, calling itself 'Little Paris', and its dried-up river bed that still 'flows' through the town, 'the Seine'. One of its merchant ships even bombarded the former capital. Highly political, its inhabitants sparked peasant revolts and uprisings against the British and made fiery fighters during the War of Greek Independence.

North of the town, at Paliokastro, very little remains of the ancient city of Pali, which flourished in the third century BC when it was colonized by

Left:
The beautiful beach of Anti Samos to the south-east of Sami

Right:
Lake Avitho,
between Poros and
Sami, was once
thought to be
bottomless by the
locals

Opposite:
**View of Argostoli
and Trapano bridge**

the Corinthians. Sadly, most of its masonry has been used at various times in the construction of Lixouri. Close by is the Monastery of Kechrionas, founded by three Cephallonians in 1694. Captured by Berber pirates, they apparently prayed to the Virgin to be returned home and awoke at this spot. The present church dates from 1828, although the chains that bound the former prisoners have been around the icon of the Virgin ever since 1694, in remembrance of this miracle.

South of Lixouri is Lepeda beach where a sunbathing Gunther Weber first encounters his friend Captain Corelli and the truckload of partying Italians and their whores in *Captain Corelli's Mandolin*. Close also is the abandoned Agia Paraskevi cave and Monastery of Aghios Anthimos, where the blind monk and hermit Anthimos Kourouklis lived and prayed between trips to the Dodecanese and Cyclades where he established several monasteries on isolated islands such as Kastellorizo and Sikinos.

West of here, at Cape Aghios Georgios, there are some impressive beaches, such as Megas Lakos and red-sanded Xi (also known as Ammoudia), all with views towards Vardiani island. Further south, at Cape Akrotiri, there is the famous rock of Kounopetra. This massive stone used to rock to and fro even when people sat on it, making twenty movements per minute, until the 1953 earthquake stopped the mysterious movements that had puzzled geologists for years.

With stunning views across the Ionian Sea, the mountainous west coast's inaccessible cliffs and caves are interspersed with empty beaches, such as Petani and Aghios Spyridon at the northernmost tip of the Paliki peninsula. There are the ruins of the Monastery of Tafion, built amidst the remains of ancient Taphios, mentioned frequently by Homer, and nearby the Monastery of Kipourion. Founded in 1759 by the monk Chrisanthos, it once had eighty monks living there. In 1915 a French battleship, mistaking smoke from the kitchen chimney for an enemy ship, fired on the monastery, damaging the church. Its dramatic clifftop setting, similar to Amorgos island's Monastery of Panagia Chozoviotissai, and its views of the sunset, are its chief attractions today. Still in the process of being rebuilt after its destruction in the 1953 earthquake, it is also home to a fragment of the holy cross, donated in 1862 by the Russian prince Vladimir Dolgouroukis, and various miraculous icons. There is an arduous walk to the Drakondi cave, forty metres deep, from the monastery.

There are only a few villages in the northern part of the Paliki peninsula, called 'Anogi' by its inhabitants, but all are picturesque examples of classic working villages. In Damoulinata, Agia Thekli and Delaporta, washing hangs from lines, donkeys bray and chickens wander freely around the streets. Villagers are either in the kafeneia or working in the fields. There are always more goats than people, and they frequently lie in the middle of the roads, forcing car drivers to toot their horns. Kaminarata is famed for its folk dances, sometimes practised in the village square.

Inland, to the east, an important Mycenaean tomb was found at Kontogenada in 1930. The Monastery of Koronatou, just three kilometres from Lixouri, was established in the fifteenth century, and its icon of the Virgin is called the *Dakryrousa* because it is reputed occasionally to shed tears. Although it is hard to believe the number of miracles that have apparently occurred on Cephallonia, when one enters these sometimes remote monasteries and villages, where life has been continuously shaped by historical events and natural disasters, it is easy to understand why religion plays such an important role in island life.

Opposite:
The white cliffs of Spartia beach on the south coast

146

Byron on Cephallonia

On 13 July 1823, twelve years after his first tour of Greece with John Cam Hobhouse, his fellow Cambridge student and faithful travelling companion, Lord Byron boarded the brig *Hercules* in the Italian port of Genoa. Depressed by the death of his six-year-old daughter Allegra in 1822, ostracized by English society, and disgusted by his narcissistic life in Italy, Byron had been thrown a lifeline when the newly formed London Greek Committee had appointed him as their representative. At last, he could involve himself in a worthwhile cause again, and the Greeks who struggled for independence were to give him a hero's welcome when he arrived in Cephallonia. Accompanied this time by his friend Edward John Trelawny he observed on the voyage: 'I was happier in Greece than I have ever been before – or since.'

The *Hercules* sailed into Argostoli harbour on 3 August, with Byron invigorated by the sea voyage and 'in excellent health and good humour'. Among his first visitors were a group of Suliote refugees to whom he gave funds to return to Roumeli. After a reception in his honour, given by officers of the British Army's Eighth Royal Foot Regiment, his confidence was fully restored. Two days after his arrival, Charles Napier, the island's British governor, returned to Cephallonia and reported, in one of his letters, 'Lord Byron is here and I like him very much.'

While waiting for funds and replies to his various letters to Greek leaders, Byron, together with his companions – Trelawny, his personal physician Dr Bruno, Count Gamba and some servants – visited Ithaki. Returning to Sami by rowing boat, they spent the night at the nearby monastery of Agrillion where Byron had a famous attack of nerves. After what seemed an interminable and formal greeting by the monks, Byron rushed to one of the cells, tore up his clothes and the bedding and

smashed the meagre furniture, screaming at his companions: 'Fiends, can I have no peace, no relief from this hell! Leave me, I say.' He had to be restrained, and next morning, after begging forgiveness from the Abbot, the group left for Argostoli again, with Byron so much improved that he sang folk-songs in a Cockney accent along the road.

After the death of the Suliote leader Marko Botsaris, Byron decided to stay on the island a little longer. On 6 September, he set off for the village of Metaxata where he rented a small house. Byron insisted that the land-lady continue to light the oil lamp beneath the icon of Aghios Georgios every night in his bedroom. He found peace in this haven, writing in his journal: 'Standing at the window of my apartment in this beautiful village, the calm though cool serenity of a beautiful and transparent moonlight, showing the islands, the mountains, the sea, with a distant outline of the Morea traced between the double azure of the waves and skies, has quieted me enough to be able to write.'

A place of pilgrimage for many visitors after his death, the house was destroyed by the 1953 earthquake. Henry Napier, Charles Napier's brother, visited and wrote:

To Lord Byron's admirers this village is classic ground, for he resided there for three months previous to his going to Missolonghi and his death. In consequence of not speaking Greek I had some difficulty to find the house because, as I afterwards discovered, the inhabitants knew him by no other name than 'Milordo'. It is small but situated on one of the most retired corners of this beautiful village with a fine view of the rich plain on one side and on the other the Castle of St George and Mount Aenos.

Another pilgrimage was made in 1836 by the German botanist Furst Hermann von Pückler Muskau:

The simple house in which Childe Harold lived his last mortal hours is small and poor and set in enchantingly beautiful scenery on the highest terrace of Metaxata with a view over a green landscape to Zante and an isolated rock near the coast on which a temple to Zeus once stood. His favourite spot was by a windmill lower down by the sea, a half hour's walk, which we visited. It lies amidst vineyards and is approachable through a delightful walk shaded with centuries old olive trees whose baroque-like limbs twist over an area of 20 feet. The view from here is fantastic and Byron would sit here for hours gathering inspiration for poems of which his premature death has deprived us.

There are various amusing stories about Byron's brief stay on the island, including one of him experiencing an earthquake on 5 October. Most evenings, young and eager British officers would come to pay their respects. Sometimes, he would ride into Argostoli to discuss theology throughout the night with the regiment's doctor, James Kennedy, an ardent Methodist. On another visit to the young Dr Muir, one of his new-found friends, he refused the offer of a bed and insisted on riding home during a severe thunderstorm. Byron himself remarked:

I like this spot although I do not know the reason and I would not like to leave. Here of course there are not many attractions, neither in the comforts of my house nor the melancholy view of the Black Mountain. There are no contacts with educated persons, nor are there any beautiful women. Yet in spite of all I would like to linger because I feel more satisfied and time passes more pleasantly than ever long before.

In December, Byron left the island for Missolonghi, on board a *mistico*, a two-masted caique. He was accompanied by his trusted Dr Bruno and English servant Fletcher, a Newfoundland dog called Lyon and a young Greek boy, Lucas Chalandritsanas, who had become his page and to whom Byron dedicated his last poem. It must have been a strange sight, as Byron and his theatrical troupe finally set sail, unaware that he was soon to meet his death in tragic and unnecessary circumstances a few months later. He died in April 1824 of pneumonia. John Pitt Kennedy wrote to Charles Napier, on leave in London, on 2 April:

The melancholy news of Lord Byron's death will have reached you ere you receive this. The medical men here agree that it was entirely the fault of Doctors. He got wet which brought on inflammation of the chest. The doctors immediately proposed bleeding but he would not allow them, saying that the lancet has destroyed more men than the lance. The next morning, however, he was delirious and of course incapable of preventing their doing what they thought best, he remained delirious for several (6 or 7) days but was never bled, and everyone agrees that excessive bleeding was the only chance he would have had; his loss will be most severely felt by the Greeks although there are those among them who would impute bad motives to his exertions in their favour now that he is gone ...

Right:
An old bell in
the village of
Mazoukata behind
Argostoli

General Information

Food and Drink

Although it is often hard to find some of the unique Ionian island recipes in many of Cephallonia's tourist restaurants, they certainly exist in the repertoire of isolated village homes and humble tavernas. As with all the main Ionian islands, the legacy of Cephallonia's history of occupations is a rich variety of ingredients and cooking styles that are still found on the island. The Venetians, French and British have all left their mark. Through trade with the Spanish Empire, the Venetians introduced vegetables now widely used throughout Greece, such as the tomato, corn, beans, squash and pumpkin from the New World, as well as a love of sweet and sour recipes using currants and vinegar. The Venetian style of *en saor* cooking, where small fish are fried with onions and wine vinegar and then marinated in their cooking liquid, is still popular.

Often, this style of cooking, called *savoro* on the islands, uses wine vinegar and rosemary as the main flavourings. There is even a recipe for a pie similar to the one beloved by the Venetian and Sicilian aristocracy: *Venetzianiko pastitsio* combines macaroni, chicken livers, mortadella, roasted and minced meats, eggs, herbs and spices to produce a rich pie that is still made on special occasions. The French introduced the potato and the turkey (*gallopoula* – 'French bird') and the English have left a craving for somewhat stodgy puddings, such as *poutinga* (a type of English trifle with creme caramel).

There are several seafood and meat recipes that are said to be unique to Cephallonia. *Oktopodopitta* (octopus pie) is always eaten on the third Sunday of Lent, as part of the annual Lenten fast. There are many variations for *Kefallonitiki kreatopitta* (Cephallonian meat pie), a popular recipe that always contains lamb or goat, herbs such as marjoram, rice, potatoes and eggs, and sometimes prunes, raisins, pine nuts or almonds. Another popular island dish is *bourdetto* (a corruption of the Italian soup *brodetto*) – more stew than soup – a dish that combines fish, tomatoes and onions with cayenne or paprika.

Seafood is also widely cooked with vegetables: *Tsipoura* (gilthead bream) is braised with celery and *avgolemono* sauce; *soupies* (cuttlefish) with celery and garlic; *barbounia* (red mullet) with *seskoula* (Swiss chard). Game is also utilized in imaginative ways: partridge pilaff; pigeon with broad beans; rabbit or hare *lagoto*, an unusual stew with tomatoes, garlic and lemon juice. As in all the Ionian islands, *sofrito* (veal braised with garlic, parsley and vinegar) and *pastitsada* (a veal, garlic and wine ragout with pasta) are also popular dishes. Wild greens are picked and used for pies and for *tsigarelli* (sautéed greens with potatoes and herbs); *paximathia* (double-baked dried bread) is softened in water and then made into salads that combine garlic, oregano, olive oil and vinegar. Another speciality with Italian roots is home-made egg noodles, such as *toumatsi*, grated into small pieces and used in soups and stews.

The origins of Robola wine have been traced to the Friuli region, north-east of Venice, when the local ribola grape was planted on the island by Venetian colonists. Today, Cephallonia is the only island to be awarded the right to three appellation of origin (*'appellation d'origine contrôlée'*) entitlements for its Robola, Mavrodaphne and Muscat wines.

Where to eat traditional
Cephallonian cuisine

Argostoli
Taverna Patsouras
Telephone: 0671 22779

Kaliva Restaurant
Telephone: 0671 24168

Stateri
Telephone: 0671 25438

Casa Grec
Telephone: 0671 24091

Paraktion
Telephone: 0671 22510

Fiskardo
Tassia
Telephone: 0674 41205

Skala
Paspalis
Telephone: 0671 83140

Light House
Telephone: 0671 81355

Left:
**Artichokes for sale
in Argostoli**

Museums

Archaeological Museum
Rokkou Vergoti street
Argostoli
Telephone: 0671 28300
Open Tuesday to Sunday.
Closed public holidays.

Corgialenios Museum
Historical and folk museum
Ilia Zervou 12
Argostoli
Telephone: 0671 28835
Open April to October, Monday to
Saturday. Closed public holidays.

Typaldon Iakovatos Museum
Lixouri
Tel. / fax: 0671 91325

Where to stay

Traditional mansions:
Erissos
Fiskardo
Telephone: 0674 41327
Open May to October.
180-year-old building with four
rooms.

Filoxenia
Fiskardo
Tel. / fax: 0674 41319
Open April to November.
Located near the old harbour, this
elegant building was built in 1766
to house the local Venetian
administration. There are now six
rooms.

Ionian Plaza
Argostoli
Telephone: 0671 25581

Mouikis
Argostoli
Telephone: 0671 23454 / 6

Mirabel
Argostoli
Telephone: 0671 25381 / 3

Tara Beach
Skala
Telephone: 0671 83341 / 3

Pericles
Sami
Telephone: 0674 22780 / 5

Sami Beach
Sami
Telephone: 0674 22802

Bibliography

Ansted, D.T. *The Ionian islands in the year 1863*, London, W.H. Allen, 1863

Cervi, Mario, *The Hollow Legions, Mussolini's Blunder in Greece 1940–1941*, New York, Doubleday, 1971

Cosmetatos, Helen, *The Roads of Cefalonia*, Argostoli, Corgialanos Museum, 1995

De Bernières, Louis, *Captain Corelli's Mandolin*, London, Minerva, 1995

Ghilardini, Padre Luigi, *I Martiri di Cefalonia*, Editrice Ligure

Holland, Henry, *Travels in the Ionian Islands and Albania in 1812 and 1813*, London, 1815

Jervis White, *Henry, History of the Island of Corfu and of the Republic of the Ionian Islands*, London, Colburn and Co., 1852

Kirkwall, Viscount, *Four years in the Ionian islands*, London, Chapman and Hall, 1864

Louis, Diana Farr, and Marinos, June, *Prospero's Kitchen, Mediterranean cooking of the Ionian Islands*, New York, M. Evans and Co., 1995

Marinatos, Spyridon, *Cephalonia*, Cephallonia, T.E.T, 1962

Napier, Charles James, *The Colonies: treating of their value generally – of the Ionian islands in particular*, London, Thomas and William Boone, 1833

Partsch, Joseph, *Kephallenia und Ithaka, Eine Geographische Monographie*, Breslau University, 1890

Petris, Tasos, *Cephalonia, Toubis Guide*, Toubis Guide, Athens, 1995

Ravanis, George D., *Byron in Cephalonia*, Cephallonia, Corgialenios Foundation, 1982

Venturi, Marcello, *The White Flag*, London, Anthony Blond, 1966

Index

Note: Page numbers in *italic type* refer to illustrations on page cited.